A LAYMAN'S GUIDE TO THE
GREEK HEROES

ALAN & MAUREEN CARTER

A LAYMAN'S GUIDE TO THE
GREEK
HEROES

EFSTATHIADIS GROUP

EFSTATHIADIS GROUP S.A.
14, Valtetsiou Str.
106 80 Athens
Tel: (01) 5254650, 6450113
Fax: (01) 5254657
GREECE

ISBN 960 226 487 X

© **Efstathiadis Group S.A. 1998**

Printed and bound in Greece

To our good friend John Townsend for his help and advice and to all our other friends who encouraged and supported us.

The authors now live in the Argolid region of the Peloponnese at Palaia Epidauros, a beautiful setting on the Eastern coast looking toward the peninsular of Methana and the islands of Aegina and Agistri.

Palaia Epidauros (Ancient Epidauros) dates back to pre-Mycenean times and was the guardian of the Sanctuary of Asclepus, which houses the world famous theatre. It was once a major city of some 80,000 inhabitants. Relatively unexcavated it has its own small theatre (circa 400 BC), temple ruins accredited to Aphrodite and Athena, Mycenean shaft graves and the sunken remains of parts of the old city.

Contents

A Guide to the Greek Heroes

Introduction

By the fourth generation of Greek Gods, we see the emergence of mortal man and of a new breed which provided the basis of countless mythological stories.

Originating from the unions of Gods and mortals, they can be said to have been half god and half human. These Heroes and Heroines, as they are called, emerged in direct contact and association with the Greek Gods and some were rewarded with immortality.

At this time all the values and emotions attributed to humans were in place and it is not too difficult to construe the exploits of the Heroes as being the practical illustrations of our now accepted human condition, although as in many other ancient civilizations, their achievements suggest an intermediary race of supermen. The thin line which separates mythology from recorded fact was bridged on many occasions by the Heroes and the brilliance of the Greek classical period (480 BC-323 BC) was heralded by their achievements and those of the Gods before them.

There is no doubting that future generations of these supermen were to give much of the western world the key to philosophy, art, science, medicine, government and architecture and it is in these fields that much of our today's vocabulary is descended from the Greek language.

The main theme of the Heroes' adventures was the assertion of good over evil and right over wrong. Wisdom, guile, strength, courage, endurance and application were demonstrated in a multitude of examples. However, the

Greek idea of a Hero didn't embrace just these qualities. His understanding of a Hero or Heroine recognised many other traits, best illustrated by Fig. No 1. These supermen were both aided and thwarted by the Gods, often being the instrument of one God's dispute with another.

What is a Hero?

Like the Gods, many of the Heroes were worshipped in their associated region of Greece and in this respect can be compared with the later veneration of the Christian saints. In the 8th century BC, both Hesiod and Homer were to provide the lineal link with the Gods and the Heroes and it was at this time that the first Olympic Games were established to seek the finest exponents of physical fitness combined with athletic skill. Track, field and physical combat events, together with chariot races, all bore a remarkable likeness to the exploits of the Gods and Heroes and at Olympia, Delphi, Nemea and Isthmia in particular, the sites were dedicated to them with various temples and statues. The throwing of the discus, shot, javelin and hammer can all be related to recorded adventures of the Gods and Heroes. It was the throw of a discus by PERSEUS that accidentally killed his grandfather and again it was a discus thrown by APOLLO that struck poor HYACINTHUS. MELEAGER was renowned for the throwing of the javelin and ARES was laid low with a shot thrown by ATHENE.

There are many written versions of the exploits of the Greek Heroes, some differing only in small details, others disagreeing in matters of lineage, place or circumstance. So we ask for your forebearance, as we have tried to choose the most logical path through the inconsistencies. There is also much that we have had to leave out, especially in the matter of the adventures of HERACLES and JASON, which would fill a book on their own, but we hope we have included the most important of their experiences.

*Note: A number alongside a name denotes that there existed more than one prominent person with that title.

Part 1
HERACLES

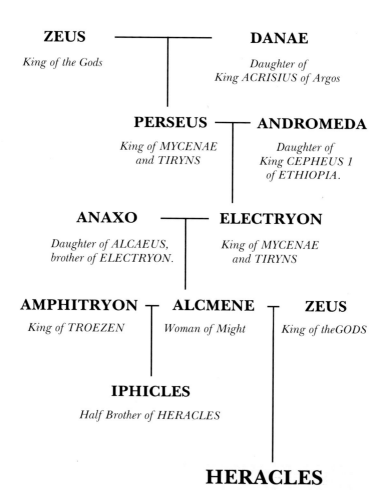

ZEUS

King of the Gods

DANAE

*Daughter of
King ACRISIUS of Argos*

PERSEUS

*King of MYCENAE
and TIRYNS*

ANDROMEDA

*Daughter of
King CEPHEUS 1
of ETHIOPIA.*

ANAXO

*Daughter of ALCAEUS,
brother of ELECTRYON.*

ELECTRYON

*King of MYCENAE
and TIRYNS*

AMPHITRYON

King of TROEZEN

ALCMENE

Woman of Might

ZEUS

King of theGODS

IPHICLES

Half Brother of HERACLES

HERACLES

HERACLES, the personification of physical strength, more popularly known by his adopted Roman name of HERCULES, was indubitably the most famous hero of all. The folklore and myths of nations all over the world have produced 'HERACLES' in one form or another. An immense character, he must surely be everone's idea of:
Strength against Weakness.
Right against Wrong.
Resolution against Indecision.
Courage against Cowardice.

Perhaps the modern James Bond was born from the legends of HERACLES!

ZEUS had decided to produce a son who could be the ultimate protector of both mortals and immortals, to rule over all Greece, an example of courage and strength and a wise counsellor to all.

He chose the genetic strain of PERSEUS, renowned for his strength and might. Both AMPHITRYON, nephew of ELECTRYON the king of Mycenae, and ALCMENE, daughter of ELECTRYON, were descended from PERSEUS and therefore were the ideal choice as parents.

ELECTRYON and his nine sons were at war with the Taphians and the Teleboans, who were claiming the Mycenaean throne and he lost eight of his sons in the battle, the only remaining son being LICYMNIUS. On the return of ELECTRYON to Mycenae, he was accidentally killed by AMPHITRYON who threw a club in anger and it rebounded from the horns of a cow, to strike a fatal blow. AMPHITRYON was banished for this deed and he left for Thebes, together with ALCMENE and LICYMNIUS.
He was welcomed in Thebes by King CREON who purified him of the unfortunate death of ELECTRYON. However, ALCMENE would not lie with her husband until he had

avenged the death of her eight brothers.

With CREON's help, AMPHITRYON raised an army and waged war on the Taphians and the Teleboans, which was successful. It was while he was thus engaged that ZEUS laid his plans. He disguised himself as AMPHITRYON, came to ALCMENE announcing his victory and laid with her all night, a night made three times its normal length with the aid of HELIOS and SELENE, God of the sun and Goddess of the moon.

Within hours the actual victor, AMPHITRYON, returned and ALCMENE was mystified by his passion which should have been quenched and by his battle tales which she had already heard. In his turn, AMPHITRYON was bemused by the lack of real passion from ALCMENE.

Nine months later, on the destined day of birth, ZEUS announced from Olympus that he would become the father of a child that day who would be called HERACLES, meaning 'Glory of HERA' who would rule the House of PERSEUS.

The boasting of the adulterous ZEUS made HERA ask that any child descended from PERSEUS, born before midnight, would become king of all Greece. Sensing no danger, ZEUS agreed and the vengeful HERA set to work. She hastened to Mycenae where NICIPPE, wife of STHENELUS, son of PERSEUS, was seven months with child and she started to bring about an early birth. She then went to Thebes and sat cross legged, with fingers locked, on ALCMENE's doorstep. She prevented the attendance of ILLYTHIA, her daughter and the Goddess of Chilbirth and therefore it was past midnight when the infant HERACLES was born.

In the meantime, NICIPPE had given birth to a seven month boy, to be called EURYSTHEUS.

ZEUS was furious at HERA'S trickery but had to stand by his promise. EURYSTHEUS was therefore destined to become the high king of the House of PERSEUS. However, ZEUS now made HERA promise that HERACLES would be elevated to a God if he performed ten tasks to be set by EURYSTHEUS, when he reached manhood.

Twenty four hours after the birth of HERACLES, ALCMENE gave birth to another boy, to be named IPHICLES, a twin to HERACLES and the son of AMPHITRYON, whose seed had been delayed by that time period.

While the tasks, to be known as Labours, were meant to qualify HERACLES for immortality, some accounts make him immortal as a child, which then gives more credence to his earliest superhuman feats. The story goes that one day, ALCMENE, guided by ZEUS, placed her baby, HERACLES, in a spot outside the walls of Thebes, where the God knew that HERA would be walking with ATHENE. When the pair came across the baby, ATHENE remarked to HERA on the healthy looking abandoned child and how she might ensure its well being being by breast feeding the infant, as HERA was with milk. HERA duly took the infant to her breast where the feeding was so fierce that HERA quickly drew away. Some say that the splash of milk became the Milky Way, but the milk from the immortal HERA had passed immortality to HERACLES.

The first sign of HERACLES strength and courage was to appear before his first birthday, when the vindictive HERA sent two large serpents to the house of AMPHITRYON, to attack the twin boys in their cot. ZEUS illuminated the nursery to alert the twins to the danger and they awoke to see the two serpents, which had flaming eyes and poison drenched fangs. The baby IPHICLES screamed as he fell to the floor, which caused AMPHITRYON and ALCMENE to hurry to the nursery. When they arrived it was to find HERACLES with a strangled serpent in each hand.

As a child, HERACLES was given the very best tuition in chariot driving, fencing, boxing, archery, music, literature, wisdom and virtue. His physical development was immense and his hunting talents supreme. He preferred the outdoor life to home comforts. His first exploit occurred when he was eighteen years of age.

The herds of his foster father and King THESPIUS were being ravaged by a lion and HERACLES joined the hunt. It happened that King THESPIUS had fifty daughters and he so admired HERACLES that he wanted them all to produce a child from him. So HERACLES was a guest of King THESPIUS, at Mount Helicon, for fifty days and nights while the lion hunt was in progress. Each night he entertained a different daughter and the king's wishes were fulfilled. As for the lion, when HERACLES eventually found it, he beat it to death with a club which he had fashioned from a wild olive tree.

The first major work of HERACLES was to rescue his native Thebes from the city of Orchomenus, which had captured it while HERACLES had been away hunting the lion at Mount Helicon. He provoked a war when he met the heralds of King ERGINOS of Orchomenus on their annual visit to collect their tribute of one hundred cattle. If the tribute was not paid, they were to cut off the hands, nose and ears from every male in Thebes. 'If that is the mind of King ERGINOS, then he will be paid', said HERACLES and he meted out the same disfigurement to the heralds and sent them back to Orchomenus. HERACLES then trained all the males of Thebes in the use of weapons. The oracle told him that he would succeed against Orchomenus, provided that the noblest man of Thebes would take his own life. Now this was one ANTIPOENUS, and when he refused to die for the common good, his two daughters, ANDROCLEIA and ALCIS, took his place and were honoured thereafter as the Heroines of Thebes.

Following the return of his heralds, King ERGINOS marched on Thebes but HERACLES ambushed his army in a narrow pass, killing the king and his senior aides. Having defeated the army, he then attacked Orchomenus and captured the city.

In thanks for his victory, HERACLES established memorials to ZEUS, ARTEMIS and ATHENE at Thebes and the Thebans themselves honoured HERACLES with a statue known as HERACLES the Nose Docker in remembrance of his treatment of the heralds.

The fame of HERACLES was spreading. CREON was now king of all the new region and HERACLES was given CREON's daughter, MEGARA, in marriage. The pair lived many peaceful years in Thebes and had eight children. The union, however, was to end unhappily. The jealous HERA, determined to do all in her power to destroy HERACLES, sent LYSSA, the Fury of Madness, to impart her terrible gift of derangement to HERACLES. As soon as he was afflicted by the malady, he perceived his whole family as his enemies and in his madness killed them all, including two sons of his twin brother. IPHICLES, however, saved his eldest son, IOLAUS, by removing him in time. HERACLES was about to kill his father, AMPHITRYON, when the Goddess ATHENE intervened, throwing a stone which hit HERACLES on the chest and he fell into a deep sleep. When he woke, he was cured of his mania and saw the terrible thing he had done.

Seeking to purge himself of the dreadful act, HERACLES sought advice from the oracle at Delphi, which instructed him to go to the Argolid and there undertake the ten labours that would be set by King EURYSTHEUS. Thus the basis of the agreement between ZEUS and HERA, that should he be successful, he would take up his place on Olympus as a God, was realised. As we shall see, King EURYSTHEUS did not recognise two of the labours and HERACLES was given two extra tasks to carry out.

So began twelve years of service to King EURYSTHEUS that would produce the famed twelve Labours of HERACLES, throughout which he would receive a good measure of advice and help from ATHENE, surely his protectress.

The Twelve Labours of HERACLES.

No 1- The NEMEAN LION

This lion was a monster offspring of TYPHON and ECHIDNE and as you will read, our Heroes have to deal with several more of the unpleasant children of this ugly couple. The lion was terrorizing the area around Nemea, which lies between Mycenae and Corinth. The labour was to kill the lion and bring the pelt back, as proof, to EURYSTHEUS. However, the monster had a skin which could resist any weapon.

When HERACLES found the lion, he failed to pierce it with his arrows and neither his sword, nor the club, which he had fashioned out of a wild olive tree, had any effect. After these attempts on its life, the beast ran for its lair, a cave in the mountain, with two entrances. HERACLES blocked one entrance with great rocks and entered the cave by the other, coming face to face with the lion, which let out a roar which shook the whole mountain, as man and beast surveyed each other for an instant. There followed a gigantic wrestling match, in which HERACLES lost a finger before he got his arm around the lion's neck, squeezing until froth and blood dripped from its mouth and eventually draining the breath from the beast.

The Nemean Lion

How to undertake the removal of the pelt? HERACLES found that the only tools up to the task were the claws of the lion itself, which were razor sharp. The complete pelt became HERACLES' garb from henceforth and when he returned to Tiryns wearing the skin with the lion's head sitting on his own, he must have looked a fearsome sight. So much so, that EURYSTHEUS took refuge in a large bronze jar, saying that he would issue further labours without coming into contact with HERACLES.

No 2 - THE HYDRA OF LERNA

This was another offspring of TYPHON and ECHIDNE. A servant to HERA, it lived in a grove in the marshes of Lerna, about 8km west of Argos, on the coast. The surrounding area was devoid of crops or cattle, which had been devastated by the beast. The HYDRA was a terrible sight. It was a huge serpent with nine heads and a dog-like body. One head was immortal and the others doubled in number if severed.
Furthermore, flames shot from its mouths and poisonous breath poured from its nostrils. Even while it slept, everything around was burned or destroyed.

Accompanied by his nephew, IOLAUS, who drove the chariot, HERACLES arrived at Lerna. ATHENE was on hand to advise him and after driving the monster from its lair with burning arrows, he held his breath and wrestled with it. With a sickle he began to cut off the beast's heads, but as fast as he cut, they multiplied. The HYDRA twisted one of its necks around the foot of HERACLES and then a huge crab, coming to the aid of the HYDRA, gripped the other foot of the Hero in its great pincers. HERACLES had to call to IOLAUS, who had stayed with the chariot, for assistance, but in the meantime he managed to crush the crab with his foot. IOLAUS came to his assistance and set fire to the grove. As HERACLES clubbed a head from the serpent, IOLAUS would sear the wound with a blazing torch. This prevented the heads from growing. Only the immortal head was left, which HERACLES severed with his sword and, with it still hissing, buried it deep in the ground, covering it with large rocks. Disembowelling the body, he dipped his arrows in the poisonous entrails and in the future they would prove fatal to any enemy.

In recognition of its vain efforts, HERA placed the crab

under the sign of Cancer in the Zodiac.
EURYSTHEUS would not recognize this feat because he
claimed that HERACLES had been unfairly assisted by
IOLAUS.

No 3- THE CERYNEIAN HIND

The third labour was to capture this hind and bring it alive
to Tiryns. The deer had golden horns, roamed the Argolid
region and was sacred to ARTEMIS. Its chief characteristic
was its ability to run so fast that no-one could catch it.

HERACLES hunted the hind for a whole year, chasing it
up mountains, across valleys, through forests and by lakes.
At last it seemed as if the hind was tiring, but still
HERACLES could not catch up with it. Eventually the
animal came to the banks of the river Ladon in Arcadia,
and plunging into the water, began to swim for the
opposite bank. HERACLES reached the river and made a
decision to risk wounding the hind. He took an arrow from
his quiver and shot. The hind reached the bank, wounded
and exhausted. HERACLES lost no time, swam across and
caught the golden horned animal, placed it over his
shoulders and set out on his return journey. On the way he
met APOLLO and ARTEMIS. The capture of the hind
angered ARTEMIS and she would have released it, but
relented when HERACLES explained that EURYSTHEUS
was to blame. On his arrival at Tiryns, HERACLES was sent
immediately to capture, alive, a wild boar, which was to be
his next labour.

No 4 - THE ERYMANTHIAN BOAR

This meant a return to Arcadia, where the huge beast lived
on Mount Erymanthus, ravaging the area around. On his
way, HERACLES met the Centaur, PHOLUS, and was
entertained to a meal and wine. Unfortunately, living

nearby, were less civilised fellow Centaurs of PHOLUS; those who, as you will read, had been driven out from Mount Pelion by THESEUS after they had violated the Lapith women. They became madly drunk on just the smell of the wine being imbibed by HERACLES and PHOLUS, and they tried to steal it. A great brawl ensued and HERACLES drove them back to their home on Mount Malea. On his return he found that poor PHOLUS had been examining HERACLES' arrows when one fell on his foot and the HYDRA's venom killed him instantly.

HERACLES finally tracked down the boar on Mount Erymanthus. He had to find the right way to accost the creature, as there was great danger from its terrible teeth and yet, if he fought too hard, he might kill it, and his task was to take it alive. So HERACLES climbed the mountain to the place where the boar lived and let out a great shout. The frightened animal threw itself out of the clump of undergrowth where it was lying, but HERACLES did nothing except utter a great roar again. The animal ran, with HERACLES shouting behind it. Continuing in this manner, the Hero drove the wild boar forward until it fell into deep snow. Here it exhausted itself in its attempts to go on until HERACLES was able to capture it with a noose which he had prepared beforehand. He tied its feet and hoisting it onto his shoulders, began his return journey.

It was during this time that HERACLES heard about JASON and his forthcoming quest for the Golden Fleece. He offered his services and sailed with the Argo under JASON, but events of which you will read later forced him to leave the ship on the outward journey, at Mysia.

Returning to resume his labours, HERACLES found that EURYSTHEUS was angry at his temporary defection with

JASON and had therefore made his next labour a humiliating task.

No 5 - THE AUGEIAN STABLES

King Augeis of Elis had many cattle which, over the years, had produced a deep layer of dung over both his stables and the surrounding land, making the stables unmanageable and the ground impossible to plough. EURYSTHEUS gave HERACLES the task of clearing away the accumulated excrement. HERACLES went to King AUGEIS and, not informing him of his allotted labour, offered to clean the stables and land in just one day, for a payment of one tenth of the king's cattle. The king agreed and the deal was witnessed by PHYLEUS, the son of King AUGEIS.

HERACLES then broke through the supporting bank of the river Menius, diverting its flow such that the stables and the surrounding land were directly in its path. The dung was washed away and then the breach filled. However, AUGEIS refused payment, having learnt that it was a labour imposed by EURYSTHEUS, and when PHYLEUS supported HERACLES in his claim, the king put his son into exile.

EURYSTHEUS discounted this labour because HERACLES had sought to gain from his punishment.

No 6 - THE STYMPHALIAN BIRDS

The Marshes of Stymphalia lie in the north east of Arcadia and were populated by a colony of awesome birds which had beaks, claws and wings of metal. They fed on humans and were so large and numerous that when they collectively took flight, the area was darkened, as the sun was blotted out. The sixth labour of HERCULES was to rid the marshes of these gruesome birds. ATHENE gave him a pair of brass cymbals, which had been fashioned by HEPHAESTUS, and advised him to stand on a high spot and clash them. They produced a terrifying sound which caused the birds to take flight, whereupon HERACLES, wasting no time, let loose arrow after arrow and killed many. The rest, frightened by the noise, fled to a remote island where later, it is said, the Argonauts found them.

All of the labours of HERACLES to date had been local to the Peloponnese and he had performed them with relative ease. EURYSTHEUS now decided to increase the risk element and send HERACLES abroad, which led him to Crete.

No 7 - THE CRETAN BULL

King MINOS of Crete had been given a bull by POSEIDON, in order that he might sacrifice the animal in honour of the God. When MINOS failed to do so, POSEIDON maddened the bull, which escaped from the palace and lived wild around Knossos, doing great harm to the surrounding area. So great was its frenzy that flames came from its mouth. It was this bull which had fathered the Minotaur on the king's wife, Queen PASIPHAE.

EURYSTHEUS gave to HERACLES the task of capturing the wild bull and bringing it back to Tiryns alive. HERACLES travelled to Crete and at the palace of Knossos he asked permission from King MINOS to hunt the bull. King MINOS agreed, although he doubted it was possible, considering the wild state of the animal. HERACLES set out, taking his club and a rope. He hunted the bull successfully and managed to catch it by its horns, passing a noose over its nose and around its right foot, so that it could not move. He shouldered it and carried it to Knossos, where he bade farewell to MINOS and set out for the

Peloponnese. For part of the journey he sat on the back of the bull which swam, taking him to the eastern shore of the Peloponnese, where he once more shouldered it and on reaching Tiryns, gave it to EURYSTHEUS. The bull was released and it fled to Marathon where it later terrorized that region and became the target of another great Hero, THESEUS.

The Cretan Bull

No 8 - THE MARES OF DIOMEDES

DIOMEDES, son of ARES, was the king of Thrace and the
Bistare people. He owned four mares which he fed with
human flesh. HERACLES task was to bring the mares to
Tiryns.

Accompanied by his young companion, ABDERUS,
HERACLES first overcame the grooms and drove the
horses to the seashore. The Bistares, led by DIOMEDES,
came in pursuit and HERACLES left ABDERUS in charge
of the four mares while he repelled the followers. He was
more than a match for the king and his men, with his club
and arrows forcing them to retreat, capturing DIOMEDES.
On his return, he found that poor ABDERUS had been
almost devoured by the mares in his absence. In his rage he
fed DIOMEDES to the horses, which had the effect of
quenching their thirst for human blood. HERACLES
buried the remains of ABDERUS and on that spot was
founded the city of Abdera. HERACLES returned to Tiryns
with the now tranquil mares and they were presented to
Argos as a tribute to HERA.

No 9 - THE GIRDLE OF HIPPOLYTE

For the next labour, EURYSTHEUS required HERACLES
to bring him HIPPOLYTE's girdle as a present for his
daughter, ADMETE. HIPPOLYTE was the famed queen of
the AMAZONS, a tribe of women in Asia, who mainly
fought on horseback, with exceptional ferocity and bravery.
Her soverign embellishment was a magnificent girdle given
to her by her father.

HERACLES recruited several heroes, including THESEUS,
TELEMON and PELEUS and sailed for the Black Sea
where the AMAZONS lived on its southern shore (modern
day Turkey). On arrival he was met by HIPPOLYTE, who
surprisingly offered him the girdle without resistance.

All would have been well but for the continued vengeance of HERA, who disguised herself as an AMAZON and started a rumour that HERACLES was there to abduct their queen. THESEUS fell in love with HIPPOLYTE, leading to her capture, as we will read in the exploits of that Hero, and it was she who warned HERACLES of the forthcoming attack by the roused AMAZONS. Armed with this foreknowledge, HERACLES' party defeated the women and with the belt in his possession, they began their return journey, going via Troy, where King LAOMEDON requested the help of HERACLES.

The story goes that, as a punishment from ZEUS, both POSEIDON and APOLLO had been sentenced to build the city walls of Troy for King LAOMEDON. When the task was completed, the king refused to make any payment for the work and POSEIDON took his revenge by sending a sea monster to threaten the city. APOLLO sent a plague. King LAOMEDON had consulted the oracle about his predicament, only to be told that the plague would end when he offered his daughter, HESIONE, to the sea monster, which would then itself be appeased. HESIONE was therefore chained to a rock to await her fate. HERACLES agreed to help the king and save his daughter. For payment, the king was to give him the beautiful mares which had been a present from ZEUS when the God had taken the handsome young boy, GANYMEDE from Troy, to be his personal assistant.

HERACLES had a long fight with the monster, occasionally taking refuge on a wall, provided by ATHENE. Finally he killed it but was refused his reward by LAOMEDON. Unfortunately, HERACLES did not have a sufficient force to take TROY, so he sailed away forecasting future vengeance to be heaped upon the city.
There were more minor incidents before he again reached

Tiryns, the most noteworthy being at Torone, in Sithonia, where he was challenged to a wrestling match by the two sons of PROTEUS, namely POLYGONUS and TELEGONUS. They both perished at his hands.

The belt of HIPPOLYTE was finally delivered to EURYSTHEUS and HERACLES was ready for his next labour.

No 10 - THE CATTLE OF GERYON

EURYSTHEUS next assigned HERACLES to go to Erythrea (nowadays the Cadiz area of western Spain), where the monstrous triple bodied King GERYON reigned. His labour was to bring back a valuable herd of red oxen belonging to GERYON, which were guarded day and night by a herdsman named EURYTION and the two headed hound, ORTHRUS, yet another monstrous offspring of TYPHON and ECHIDNE.

Orthrus

HERACLES travelled by way of north Africa, and when he reached the Straits of Gibraltar, he established the famed 'Pillars of HERACLES', identified now as the mountains on either side of the Straits (the Jebel Musa on the Moroccan side and the Rock of Gibraltar on the Spanish side). Arriving in Erythrea, HERACLES soon located the oxen and disposed of both EURYTION and the dreaded ORTHRUS with his club. He was leaving with the cattle when GERYON arrived to stop him. HERACLES shot him with his famous poisoned arrows and made good his escape.

The journey back with the stolen oxen was fraught with dangers as he passed through modern day southern Europe. He was attacked in Liguria (Marseilles today) by two sons of POSEIDON who attempted to steal the cattle. HERACLES killed them, only to face the entire Ligurian army. ZEUS came to his assistance, providing ammunition in the form of boulders, which HERACLES hurled at the Ligurians and which are still in evidence today on the plains west of Marseilles.

He encountered a fierce giant, CACUS, when near Rome. CACUS terrorized the surrounding region, so when HERACLES killed the giant, he became a locally revered Hero.

At the southern tip of Italy, the prize bull of the herd escaped and swam to Sicily. HERACLES, leaving his herd in the protection of HEPHAESTUS, followed the bull all the way to the western tip of Sicily, ERYX, modern day ERICE, only to be confronted by King ERYX, a famed boxer and wrestler. HERACLES demanded the return of the bull but ERYX wagered his kingdom and hence the bull, should he be defeated by HERACLES in a series of contests. After the third contest, ERYX lay dead and HERACLES left with the bull, unable to benefit from the lands of ERYX.

On his return to Tiryns with the cattle, they were sacrificed to HERA.

NO - 11 THE GOLDEN APPLES OF THE HESPERIDES

These valuable apples, which had once been a wedding present to HERA from GAIA, grew in an orchard on the land at the ends of the earth. There, they were tended by the daughters of ATLAS and HESPERUS, known as the HESPERIDES, and guarded by LADON, a huge serpent with one hundred heads.

HERACLES' task was to take the apples to EURYSTHEUS at Tiryns. The first hurdle was to establish the location of this distant land. The place was known to NEREUS, the old sea God, whom HERACLES held captive until he gave the required information.

HERACLES' journey took him by way of the Caucasus mountains, where some say he found the long suffering PROMETHEUS, who, chained to a rock, could not prevent the daily gorging of his liver by an eagle. This punishment, from ZEUS, was eternal, as PROMETHEUS' liver grew back each day.

HERACLES killed the eagle with his poisoned arrows and freed PROMETHEUS who, when he knew the task of HERACLES, advised him to send ATLAS instead.

HERACLES, however, continued his journey and he next passed through Egypt, where he was detained by King BUSIRIS. At that time, it was the policy of this king to sacrifice strangers to his country, each year, to ZEUS, if the land was to be spared from famine. Indeed, HERACLES had reached the sacrificial altar before he burst his chains asunder and killed both BUSIRIS and his son.

Next, in Libya, he met ANTAEUS, a son of GAEA. He was an immensely strong giant, who forced strangers to wrestle with him before killing them. His extraordinary strength and power came from his mother earth, such that each time

his body came into contact with the ground,
during a contest, he received a fresh charge
of energy.

In the early stages of the wrestling match
that followed, HERACLES soon realised
that each time he threw ANTAEUS to the
ground, the giant grew stronger. The end
came for ANTAEUS when HERACLES
lifted the giant's feet from contact with the

*The Golden Apples
of the Hesperides*

earth and crushed him to death in a bear hug. Moving westward, he came to ATLAS, who stood supporting the Universe on his shoulders. Remembering the advice of PROMETHEUS, he offered to shoulder the load if ATLAS would retrieve the golden apples. ATLAS agreed, but when he returned with the fruit, he said that he preferred the new arrangement and that he himself would return the apples to EURYSTHEUS.

HERACLES appeared to be in an unfortunate position, but then worked out a strategy. While continuing to support the Universe, he requested that ATLAS at least let him place a cushion on his head to ease the weight. He further asked ATLAS to hold the load for a few seconds while he got the cushion and the unthinking ATLAS readily agreed.

The moment that ATLAS took the load, HERACLES picked up the apples and left ATLAS as he had originally found him. He took the apples to Tiryns, where EURYSTHEUS let him keep them. However, HERACLES dedicated them to ATHENE, who returned them to their rightful home with the HESPERIDES.

No 12 - THE JOURNEY TO THE UNDERWORLD TO BRING BACK CERBERUS

CERBERUS was the monstrous hound of hell that guarded the gates to HADES. An offspring of TYPHON and ECHIDNE, it was the brother of the HYDRA, ORTHRUS and the NEMEAN LION. It had three heads and the tail of a serpent.

EURYSTHEUS gave this final labour to HERACLES in desperation, having failed to kill him with the previous eleven tasks.

HERACLES sought the guidance of HERMES, and after

initiation into the Eleusian Mysteries (you may remember the association of Eleusis with the Olympian Goddess DEMETER, whose daughter PERSEPHONE became the seasonal wife of HADES, who ruled the Underworld), he descended with HERMES, entering at Cape Taenarum, in the southern Peloponnese. Making their way towards the gates of Hell, before the retreating shades of the dead, they came across THESEUS and his companion PEIRITHOUS, who were bound in the chairs of forgetfulness following their unsuccessful exploit to remove PERSEPHONE. HERACLES freed THESEUS but was prevented from freeing PEIRITHOUS by an earthquake. He then released ACALAPUS (the betrayer of PERSEPHONE to HADES, when she ate the pomegranate seeds which eternally bound her to HADES) from captivity by removing the boulder which had been placed over him.

HERACLES then severely wounded MENOETES, the herdsman of HADES, who was protecting his cattle when HERACLES took one to give its blood to the thirsty shades of the dead.

Some say that HERACLES even fought with HADES, but it is more commonly believed that HADES agreed to HERACLES taking CERBERUS, provided that he could do so with his bare hands. HERACLES wrestled with the monster and finally dragged it by the scruff of its necks, back to earth.

So EURYSTHEUS had no option but to recognise the success of HERACLES. Telling him to return CERBERUS to the Underworld, he freed the Hero from any further servitude. Furthermore, as he had completed the twelve labours instructed by the Delphic Oracle, HERACLES was now assured of his reward of eventual immortality. It is possible that, with ZEUS as a father and having suckled milk from the breast of HERA, he was already immortal,

but while he remained on earth he was to
be subject to many more trials and
tribulations.

HERACLES did not return to Thebes, his
home, wishing to forget the unfortunate
past and start again. It came to his notice
that King EURYTUS of Oechalia was
offering his daughter's hand in marriage to
the man that could outshoot him and his
sons in an archery contest, so he decided to
take part.

There was no finer archer than
HERACLES, so it was really no contest, but
the king refused to give his daughter to him
in marriage, having been reminded of the
earlier shame of HERACLES,when, in his
fit of madness, he had killed his wife,

MEGARA, and their children. HERACLES left the kingdom, assuring EURYTUS of future vengeance.It is interesting to note that HERACLES was supported and trusted, at this time, by IPHITUS,the elder son of EURYTUS, but repaid the trust in a cruel revenge on the father. When IPHITUS paid a visit to HERACLES, at his home in Tiryns, he was dashed to death by the Hero, from the walls of the city.

As a result, HERACLES was inflicted with a terrible disease.In desperation he sought advice from the oracle, but the prophetess would not see him. In his anger, HERACLES stole the sacred tripod and there followed the famous encounter with APOLLO, when a struggle was only averted by ZEUS himself, who intervened and restored the tripod to its rightful place.

The Oracle now forecast that the disease would only be cured if HERACLES sold himself into bondage for three years and gave the proceeds of his labour to the surviving sons of IPHITUS.So began three years of servitude. HERACLES became the servant of OMPHALE, the queen of Lydia, in Asia Minor. During this time he went to rid Lydia of the CERCOPES. These were two dwarfish monsters, PASSALUS and ACMON, who were noted for their thieving. Some say that they were pygmies and others that they were small apes.

Their thieving was a nuisance, so HERACLES captured them, tying their feet to a pole and carrying the pole over his shoulder. Now the CERCOPES had been warned by their mother not to be caught by Blackbottom. It was when hanging from the pole that the little monsters saw the hairy body and rear of HERACLES and began to laugh. The incident so amused HERACLES that he set them free. SYLEUS of Aulis was a Lydian outlaw who was the owner of a large vineyard. He made passers by enter and dig his land for him. HERACLES killed both SYLEUS and his daughter with the garden hoe that they used.

Lydia had been threatened by its neighbouring city of Itoni for some time and HERACLES razed the city to the ground. He then rid the area of a massive serpent which had terrorised the people and damaged the crops.

Queen OMPHALE was so pleased with HERACLES' achievements that she released him from slavery and it is said by some that she bore him a son, LAMUS. He is also said to have had another son, CLEODAETUS, by one of the slave girls.

During this period he had been restored to health and it was on his return to Greece that he discovered the dead body of poor ICARUS who, you will later learn, had flown too close to the sun with his home made wings of wax, thus melting them and dropping to his death off the island of Doliche. HERACLES gave ICARUS a proper burial and called the island Icaria, in honour of the boy.

HERACLES now began a campaign of revenge against those who had previously treated him shoddily. His first target was LAOMEDON, who had cheated him of his reward when he had rescued HESIONE from the sea monster. HERACLES chose King TELAMON of Salamis as his deputy and together they took a fleet of ships on a mission to sack Troy. The walls of Troy were breached by TELAMON, who was about to enter, when his courageous action had the unwelcome effect of insulting his chief, HERACLES, whose personal honour would not allow anyone to enter before him. Indeed HERACLES would surely have struck his friend and ally but for the quick thinking TELAMON, who built a mound of bricks from the breach and announced it to be an altar, dedicated to 'our glorious victor, HERACLES'. This pleased the Hero and together they entered Troy. HERACLES killed LAOMEDON and his offspring, with the exception of HESIONE and one son named PODARCES. HERACLES took the mares, which were his original fee, plus many captives, including HESIONE, to whom he gave permission to save one captive. She chose to save her brother PODARCES, who remained as the next king of Troy, taking the name 'PRIAM' (a form of the verb 'to buy'). HESIONE became the concubine of TELAMON, the union producing a son called TEUCER.

HERACLES, still flattered and pleased by the action of his friend TELAMON, asked ZEUS to bless his marriage with a special son. ZEUS acknowledged by sending an eagle and TELAMON and his wife EURIBOEA had a glorious son called AJAX after the eagle.

If HERACLES was bent on vengeance, then so was the consistent HERA, who now sent terrible storms to trouble the return of HERACLES' fleet. They were driven to the island of Cos, where they were mistaken for pirates. The ensuing battle gave HERACLES the city when he killed King EUROPHYLUS in a decisive battle.

At this time a war was raging between the Gods and the Giants. Throughout his exploits, HERACLES had received help and guidance from the Gods, mainly from ATHENE and HERMES, from ZEUS himself and often from HEPHAESTUS (but never from HERA). An oracle had stated that the Gods would need the assistance of a mortal if they were to finally defeat the Giants. Obviously HERACLES had been groomed for this important role and so it was that in the midst of the battle, ATHENE came to him and asked him to join them on the plains of Phlegra, which was located in western Thrace. The impact of HERACLES on the war was immediate, when, together with APOLLO, they disposed of EPHIALTES, letting fly an arrow to each of the Giant's eyes. However the main obstacle was the Giant ALCYONEUS, who was immortal within the boundaries of his native land, Pallene, a region of Phlegra. HERACLES shot ALCYONEUS, then dragged him outside the boundaries of Pallene, to die. The Giant, PORPHYRION was the last to die, killed by HERACLES' arrows, having first been struck down by a thunderbolt from ZEUS.

Heracles slays a Giant

The memory of HERACLES was long, so King AUGEIAS of Elis, near Arcadia, who had refused payment for the cleaning of his stables, was killed by HERACLES, who gave the throne to the exiled son, PHYLEUS.

Two kings who had refused him purification, following his killing of IPHICLES, son of EURYTUS, were to feel the full power of HERACLES' wrath. King NELEUS of Pylos and King HIPPOCOON of Sparta both died by his hand and the killing of HIPPOCOON presented him with the opportunity to re-instate the respected brother of HIPPOCOON, TYNDAREUS, to the Spartan throne. HERACLES married DEIANEIRA, the daughter of King OENEUS of Calydon, in Aetolia (mid western Greece, nowadays the region between Nafpaktos and Arta), after defeating a rival for the girl, namely the horned ACHELOUS, the river God. He helped King OENEUS to defeat his northern enemies, the Thesprotians and he probably would have settled in Calydon but for an unfortunate accident, when he killed a nephew of OENEUS during a banquet. For this he took self imposed exile and left, with DEIANEIRA.

Just after the couple left, on the way to Trachis, in south western Thessaly, they came to the river Evenus. Who should the ferryman be, but the Centaur, NESSUS, who HERACLES had expelled from Arcadia at the time of his fourth labour. While HERACLES did not need to use his services and strode across the river, he commanded NESSUS to ferry his wife across. A scream signalled HERACLES to return, in time to shoot NESSUS and stop him from raping DEIANEIRA. The wily old NESSUS, who was dying from the poisoned arrows, pretended to DEIANEIRA to be sorry for his sins and told her to take his tunic, which was soiled with his blood. Whenever she should choose to smear it onto HERACLES' tunic, it would act as a love charm. Thinking that she might soon need it, due to the promiscuity of HERACLES, she took the soiled tunic.

Wherever HERACLES went, he was sure to find that his reputation had gone before him and countless battles were fought on behalf of whoever provided a friendly welcome for his wife and himself.

At Honus in Phthiotia (a region of southern Thessaly), he was challenged to a wrestling match by CYCNUS, the son of the war God, ARES. CYCNUS was aided by ARES, so ATHENE advised HERACLES. The result? HERACLES killed CYCNUS and badly wounded ARES, who was only saved when ATHENE told HERACLES to stop.

The last exploit of HERACLES involved revenge once more. It concerned King EURYTUS of Oechalia, whom he had defeated in an archery contest, only to be denied the prize of the king's daughter, IOLE. He gathered an army and marched on Oechalia, where he had a rescounding victory, killing the king and taking IOLE as his concubine. When DEIANEIRA heard of IOLE and took into account HERACLES' recent affairs, she decided it was time to use the Centaur's tunic and give HERACLES a love potion. When HERACLES, unknowingly, donned the soiled tunic, he became the victim of his deadly armament, the HYDRA's poison, which had made every arrow a deadly missile. His agony was instantaneous. He tore off the tunic, but it was too late.

DEIANEIRA, realising the trick that had been played on her, committed suicide and HERACLES climbed to the summit of Mount Oeta, with his son, who carried out his father's instructions to build a funeral pyre. HERACLES climbed on, and because his son refused to set light to the pyre, he asked a passing shepherd, PHILOCTETES, who consented. The grateful HERACLES gave the shepherd his famous bow and arrows in return (we will hear more of PHILOCTETES).

The flames were intense and were accompanied by thunder and lightning, to be followed by an all enveloping cloud. When the cloud finally dispersed, there was no trace of the funeral pyre. HERACLES, the immortal, had gone to take up his allotted place on Olympus, where the hand of HEBE, Goddess of Youth and daughter of ZEUS, was waiting in marriage.

A special reward went to his nephew, IOLAUS, son of his twin brother, IPHICLES, who had so faithfully assisted him in his earlier labours. To IOLAUS, a gift from HEBE, went the complete renewal of his youth.

HERACLES led a quiet, contented life in Olympus, rarely coming out or issuing advice. However, he was later to appear to PHILOCTETES, the possessor of his renowned bow and arrows, and persuade him to assist the Greeks at Troy, where he struck a vital blow and killed PARIS.

Such were the achievements of this first and foremost Hero that many books could be filled with their recounting, but let this suffice as the essential story of HERACLES.

Part 2

THESEUS

HEPHAESTUS

The Smith GOD

ATTHIS

*Daughter of King
CRANAUS of ATHENS.
From her name DERIVES the
region of ATTICA.*

ERICHTHONIOS

King of ATHENS

PRAXITHEA "A"

NAIAD NYMPH

ZEUXIPPE

*NAIAD NYMPH
Sister of PRAXITHEA "A"*

PANDION 1

King of ATHENS

ERECHTHEUS

King of ATHENS

PRAXITHEA "B"

*Daughter of Phrasimus
and Diogenia*

METIADUSA

Daughter of EUPALAMUS

CECROPS

King of ATHENS

PANDION 2

King of ATHENS

PYLIA

*Daughter of King
PYLAS of MEGARA*

AETHRA

*Daughter of King
PITTHEUS of TROEZEN*

AEGEUS

King of ATHENS

THESEUS

One of the more famous Heroes, THESEUS, like HERACLES, was a slayer of monsters. He was the son of AEGEUS, king of Athens, and AETHRA, daughter of King PITTHEUS of Troezen.

King AEGEUS, who was childless even after two marriages, had visisted Delphi to consult the oracle on this matter, only to be told,
"Do not untie the mouth of your bulging wine skin until you reach Athens, lest one day you will die of grief."
Unfortunately, he could not interpret the message and, returning to Athens via Corinth, he called on the enchantress, MEDEA, who was reputed to have magical powers. He told her that, should she ever require shelter in Athens from her many enemies, she was welcome, provided that in return she ensured that he had a son.
He next visited Troezen to see the noted wise king, PITTHEUS. PITTHEUS had a daughter, AETHRA, who was betrothed to BELLEROPHON, recently disgraced and banished for murdering his brother. PITTHEUS understood the oracle and so purposely got AEGEUS drunk and bedded him with AETHRA, hoping for a result much more preferable to the possibility of a future return of BELLEROPHON. The ploy was to be successful; however, AETHRA had slept with POSEIDON on the same night that she conceived, so THESEUS had two fathers, one mortal and one a God. Like HERACLES he shared the same peculiarties of birth that made him half human and half God.

AEGEUS, unaware that AETHRA had conceived, returned to Athens, leaving behind, under a huge rock, his sword and sandals, the ancient symbols of royalty, together with his instructions that should there be a son of the union who could move the rock and claim the sword and sandals, then he was to bring them to Athens and join his father.

Throughout THESEUS' childhood, AETHRA kept the identity of his father secret and during this time in Troezen he was popularly thought to be the son of POSEIDON. When he became a young man, already showing signs of great bravery, his mother took him to the rock and revealed his father's identity and the instructions left by him. THESEUS duly moved the huge stone, recovered the sword and sandals and set out for Athens. It was on his journey that his famed exploits began.

A dangerous bandit called PERIPHETES terrorized and robbed travellers near Epidauros, but THESEUS killed him with his own brazen club which he then kept for himself.

Near Isthmia lived SINIS, a sinister murderer who killed his victims by tearing them apart between the sprung trunks of pine trees. THESEUS made SINIS suffer the same fate.

At Crommyon he tracked down and killed a fierce wild sow, some say an offspring of TYPHON and ECHIDNE, that had been attacking the local farmers and preventing them from ploughing or seeding the land.

Following the coast road, near Megara he encountered the fierce bandit SCIRON who delighted in forcing travellers to wash his feet before kicking them from the cliffs into the sea below where a large turtle awaited his next meal. THESEUS reversed the operation and SCIRON became the next meal for the turtle.

Near Eleusis he met CERCYON, the Arcadian wrestler, who challenged travellers to compete with him and crushed them to death. THESEUS proved a match for him and dashed CERCYON to his death.

At Attic Corydallus lived the father of SINIS, called POLYPEMON, who kept a lodging house containing two beds, one short and one long. Short guests were given the long bed and he would then stretch them on a rack to make them fit the bed. Tall guests were given the short bed and were cut to size. THESEUS made POLYPEMON suffer the same brutal treatment.

The journey to Athens had certainly developed THESEUS into a Hero to be reckoned with. He was purified on the bank of the river Cephissus before entering Athens, to cleanse himself from the many killings on his journey.

In the meantime, King AEGEUS, unaware that he had a son, THESEUS, had married MEDEA, by whom he had a son, MEDUS, who was expected to eventually succeed him. It was MEDEA who recognised THESEUS for who he was and, in order to protect her son's inheritance, warned AEGEUS that this stranger, THESEUS, had come to assassinate him. Inviting THESEUS to a banquet at the palace, she arranged with AEGEUS to poison his wine. The plot would no doubt have succeeded if THESEUS had not drawn his sword to cut the beef placed before him. AEGEUS recognised the sword, realised who THESEUS was and removed the poisonous wine.

MEDEA and her son MEDUS were expelled from Athens and AEGEUS rejoiced with sacrificial offerings to the Gods for uniting him with his newly found Heroic son.

THESEUS was revered throughout Athens and supported his father's authority. He sought revenge on MEDEA but she successfully hid from him by covering herself with a magic cloud.

AEGEUS had a brother PALLAS, whose fifty sons were known as the PALLANTIDS. PALLAS and his sons plotted to overthrow AEGEUS. However, their eventual attack on

Athens was foiled by THESEUS who ambushed and destroyed them.

The next exploit of THESEUS was the slaying of the wild Marathonian bull which had been causing immense damage throughout Attica. This was the bull, you may recall, that HERACLES had brought back from Crete as a result of his seventh labour.

Now we come to THESEUS' most famous task. As an annual penalty for the killing of ANDROGEUS, son of King MINOS of Crete, the Athenians were obliged, every nine years, to deliver seven virgins and seven young men to the Cretan Palace, where they were offered as food to

the monstrous Minotaur, half bull, half human, which was kept in a labyrinth. Lots were drawn to choose the young people and every nine years, Athens resounded with lamentation as families cried for their beloved children. The agreement was that the tax would stop only when one of the victims would accomplish the killing of the monster by wrestling with him in the labyrinth. THESEUS decided to have himself included the next time that seven youths were required for the sacrificial offering, determined to kill the monster.

It happened that, when the tax was due, King MINOS himself came to collect it, in a black sailed ship. THESEUS told his father to watch for the return of the ship to Athens. If white sails were raised then he was announcing his victory, but if the black sails were in evidence then it meant he had been vanquished.

During the journey to Crete, THESEUS announced himself to be a son of POSEIDON, which was, of course, true. King MINOS threw a gold ring into the sea, telling THESEUS that if he were really POSEIDON's son, then he would be able to retrieve it. THESEUS not only returned the ring but he also delivered a crown given to him by AMPHITRITE, the Nereid wife of POSEIDON. He thus gained the confidence of King MINOS, whose daughter, ARIADNE, fell in love with the Hero. It was with the help of ARIADNE that THESEUS was able to negotiate the labyrinth and destroy the Minotaur. ARIADNE, advised by DAEDELUS. the architect of the labyrinth, gave THESEUS one end of a ball of string. While she remained outside, THESEUS entered the labyrinth, trailing the string, which enabled him to return to safety after he had killed the minotaur.

ARIADNE, together with her sister, PHAEDRA, left Crete with THESEUS, only to be abandoned on the island of

Naxos, because he could not return her love. It was here that she was discovered by DIONYSOS, the God of Wine, who she married and by whom she had three sons.

The victory of THESEUS became a tragedy when , in the excitement of a joyous return, he forgot to raise the ship's white sails. His poor father, AEGEUS, seeing black sails, was overcome with grief and threw himself into the sea and drowned.

THESEUS now became king of Attica, uniting the twelve communities and he introduced a social class system. This, in fact was the inauguration of the great city of Athens, which was to become the gem of the ancient world. He established the great festival of the 'Panathenaea', a festival in honour of ATHENE, the Lesser Pantheaea being held every July and the Great Panathenaea held in the third year of each Olympiad. The festival included horse races and musicals contests. THESEUS also introduced laws and a voting system. But adventure was in his blood and numerous exploits followed.

He fought against the Amazons, some say in company with HERACLES and abducted their queen, HIPPOLYTE, by whom he had a son, HIPPOLYTUS, who was to become thehero of another tragic story.

Following the death of HIPPOLYTE he married PHAEDRA, sister of ARIADNE, who had sailed from Crete with him after he had slain the Minotaur. The story goes that he was invited by his good friend PIRITHOUS, King of the Lapiths who dwelt in Thessaly, to a banquet celebrating the king's wedding. Neighbours from the Mount Pelion area, known as the Centaurs, half horse and half man, were also invited but they became very drunk and violated the Lapith women. THESEUS marshalled the

Lapith forces and drove the Centaurs from the area, when they established a new home on the Peloponnese. By PHAEDRA, THESEUS had two sons, but they did not compare with his eldest son HIPPOLYTUS, who developed into a handsome and athletic young man with a great hunting ability. PHAEDRA became obsessed by her desire for her step-son but the passion was not returned as the young man had sworn a vow of chastity to ARTEMIS, the Goddess of hunting to whom he was dedicated. The rejected PHAEDRA hanged herself, leaving a letter to THESEUS, saying that HIPPOLYTUS had attempted to ravage her. THESEUS, believing the letter, disowned him and asked POSEIDON to punish him. HIPPOLYTUS was duly crushed to death when his chariot horses were frightened by a marine monster sent by POSEIDON.

Together with his great friend PIRITHOUS, THESEUS went to Sparta where they carried off the beautiful HELEN. He drew lots with PIRITHOUS for HELEN and won, but she was eventually rescued by her brothers, the famous DIOSCURI. (You will read of the exploits of these twins soon.)

PIRITHOUS had designs on PERSEPHONE, the queen of the underworld, and he and THESEUS embarked on a daring plan to abduct her. They succeeded in reaching the subterranean kingdom but were prevented from leaving when HADES imprisoned them in the chairs of forgetfulness and, as you have read elsewhere, it needed HERACLES to come to the rescue. Following the tragedy surrounding HIPPOLYTUS and PHAEDRA, THESEUS retired to Scyros as a guest of King LYCOMEDES who, jealous of his great achievements, murdered him. Eventually his remains came back to Athens to be housed in the sacred Theseum.

Part 3
PERSEUS

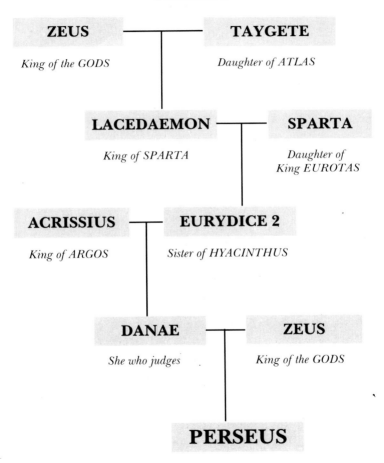

ZEUS

King of the GODS

TAYGETE

Daughter of ATLAS

LACEDAEMON

King of SPARTA

SPARTA

*Daughter of
King EUROTAS*

ACRISSIUS

King of ARGOS

EURYDICE 2

Sister of HYACINTHUS

DANAE

She who judges

ZEUS

King of the GODS

PERSEUS

PERSEUS

PERSEUS was a son of ZEUS. His mother, DANAE, had been chosen for her noble origins, as she was descended from ZEUS and TAYGETE, the daughter of ATLAS. A special result could be expected from a linking of the houses of ZEUS and ATLAS, and PERSEUS was not a disappointment. As a young man he was courageous and strong and his other heroic qualities were soon evident.

You will recall that, when ZEUS was looking for a partner with whom to father HERACLES, he chose ALCMENE, a direct descendant of PERSEUS, a genetic strain fit for extraordinary Heroes. The lineal descent chart for HERACLES clearly shows PERSEUS to be his great grandfather.

PERSEUS was conceived in the most spectacular fashion, because his mother had been locked in solitary confinement within an underground cell of bronze. This had occurred because DANAE's father, ACRISIUS, who was king of Argos, had learned from an oracle that he would meet his death from a son of his daughter.

DANAE's cell had just one small opening in the ceiling to allow a sliver of daylight to brighten her gloomy prison. ZEUS, who employed all kinds of metamorphoses in order to seduce his selected partners, this time found his way barred to human or animal forms. So he used an ingenious method to visit DANAE, entering through the aperture in the roof as a shower of gold contained within the rays of the sun.

When ACRISIUS found that a son had been born to his daughter he was both mystified and frightened. He refused to believe DANAE's account of the visit by ZEUS and decided to abandon his daughter and grandson by securely locking them in a chest, which was set adrift in the ocean.

However, under the watchful eye of ZEUS, the chest had a safe passage and was washed up on the shores of the island of Seriphus, where it was found by DICTYS, a local fisherman.

DICTYS took mother and son into his home, where PERSEUS, as the boy was called, grew to manhood and soon gathered a reputation for strength and bravery.

Now it happened that the brother of DICTYS was POLYDECTES, the king of the island, who was noted for his lusty nature. When the king saw the beautiful DANAE, he wanted her for his wife, but she was not interested and PERSEUS defended his mother's honour. Avoiding a physical confrontation, POLYDECTES falsely announced that he would seek the hand of one HIPPODAMEIA, a king's daughter. POLYDECTES required a substantial gift for such a bride and decided to ask all of his subjects to contribute horses towards the dowry.

PERSEUS owned no horses and in a moment of rashness, he offered to bring the king anything he wanted, even the head of MEDUSA, the Gorgon, although it was well known that no one had ever succeeded in returning alive from a visit to the dreaded Gorgons.

The king was happy to accept the promised head, as he knew that PERSEUS would not return, so he would be free to take DANAE as his wife.

Now PERSEUS had to match actions to words and he would have found the proposed quest impossible, had it not been for the divine protection and assistance of ATHENE and HERMES.

The Gorgons were the hideous offspring of the sea God, PHORCYS, and his sister, the sea monster, CETO. There were three of them, STHENO, EURYALE and MEDUSA, of whom only MEDUSA was mortal. Their faces were so terrible to behold that one glimpse would turn the viewer to stone. Long red tongues hung from their mouths through fearsome boars tusks and their hair writhed with snakes. Wings of gold and hands of bronze completed their awesome appearance and armour.

ATHENE advised PERSEUS to travel to Libya, where, in a cave, he would find the three sisters of the Gorgons, known as the GRAEAE. They were grey haired hags, who shared just one tooth and one eye between them. They alone had the information necessary to locate the nymphs, who possessed certain equipment essential to a confrontation with the Gorgons.
HERMES gave PERSEUS a sword and loaned his winged sandals to speed him on his way. When he located the GRAEAE, PERSEUS found them loyal to their gruesome sisters and unwilling to tell him where he could find the nymphs. He chose a moment when their one eye was being passed between them, to snatch it away and, for its safe return, they were forced to give him the required directions.

PERSEUS flew on to visit the nymphs, who readily gave him a helmet which rendered him invisible, and a large wallet with shoulder straps. Together with his own bronze shield, he was now fully equipped to meet the Gorgons. Travelling to the westernmost parts of the earth, he came to the Gorgons' cave, recognising it from the countless stone statues of those who had gazed upon the evil sisters. It was now essential that his viewing should only be from the reflection in his shield. Wearing the helmet which made him invisible, he approached the Gorgons as they lay asleep. Aiming for the mortal MEDUSA, he fixed her image in the shield and guided by ATHENE, severed the head of MEDUSA and stuffed it into the wallet. From the neck of

MEDUSA sprang the winged horse, PEGASUS, offspring of POSEIDON's union with her. PERSEUS made good his ecape, pursuit by STHENO and EURYALE being impossible, as he was still invisible. On his way back, over Africa, drops of blood fell from the severed head of MEDUSA onto the land below and became wild beasts, which filled the whole land.

PERSEUS rested, on his journey home, in the coastal region of Ethiopia, where a distant relation, King CEPHEUS, ruled. Now it so happened that, at this time, the wife of the king, namely CASSIOPEIA, had the audacity to boast of being more beautiful than the NEREID sea nymphs,

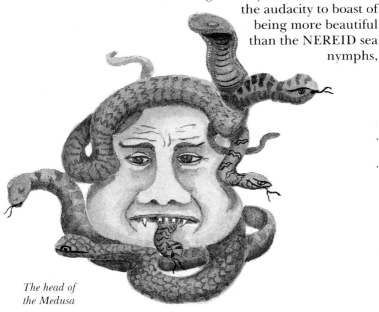

The head of the Medusa

themselves the daughters of the sea God, NEREUS. The NEREIDS complained to POSEIDON, who sent a fearsome sea monster to beleaguer the coastal area.

King CEPHEUS had consulted the oracle, to be told that he could only save his country and people if he sacrificed his beautiful daughter, ANDROMEDA, by chaining her to a rock as an offering to the monster. PERSEUS, seeing the lovely ANDROMEDA, pledged to save her and kill the monster, provided that she could become his wife and that part of CEPHEUS' kingdom would become his. With this agreement, the Hero, after a mighty struggle, slew the monster and rescued his bride.

A banquet was arranged in PERSEUS' honour, to be soured when it was learnt that CEPHEUS had failed to mention that the hand of ANDROMEDA had already been promised to his brother, PHIDEUS.
PHIDEUS and his followers came to claim ANDROMEDA, greatly outnumbering PERSEUS and his men. In the face of such odds, PERSEUS, telling his own companions to close their eyes, withdrew the head of MEDUSA from the wallet, whereupon PHIDEUS and his troops were instantly turned to stone.

After a period in Ethiopia, when a son, PERSES, was born from his marriage to ANDROMEDA, PERSEUS left his son to inherit the kingdom and returned, with his wife, to Seriphus. On arrival he found that in his absence, POLYDECTES had abducted his mother, DANAE and, going to the palace, he found the king feasting with his friends.
PERSEUS announced the success of his mission to the gathering but was not believed. So he took the Gorgon's head once more from the wallet and instantly the king and his assembled guests were turned to stone.

Returning the sandals and sword to HERMES, who agreed to deliver the helmet and wallet to the nymphs, PERSEUS finally presented the head of MEDUSA to ATHENE. It became the centre piece of her famous 'aegis', the shield fashioned from a goat's hide.

PERSEUS installed DICTYS on the throne of Seriphus and made his way, with DANAE and ANDROMEDA, to Argos, to confront his grandfather. ACRISIUS, hearing of his arrival, fled to Larisa.

Now it happened that funeral games were being held in Larisa at that time and PERSEUS, being a renowned athlete, was invited to compete. Here the oracle delivered to ACRISIUS came true, because, while he was a spectator at the games, he was struck on the forehead by a discus and died instantly. The innocent thrower of the discus was none other than PERSEUS.

In the circumstances, PERSEUS did not wish to inherit his grand father's kingdom, so instead he exchanged Argos for the throne of Tiryns. There he ruled for many years, together with ANDROMEDA, during which time the couple produced five sons and a daughter. PERSEUS founded Mycenae and this period of rule in Tiryns and Mycenae was known as the Perseid Dynasty.

On the deaths of PERSEUS and ANDROMEDA, they were given eternal fame when ATHENE placed them in the heavens as stars.

Part 4
BELLEROPHON

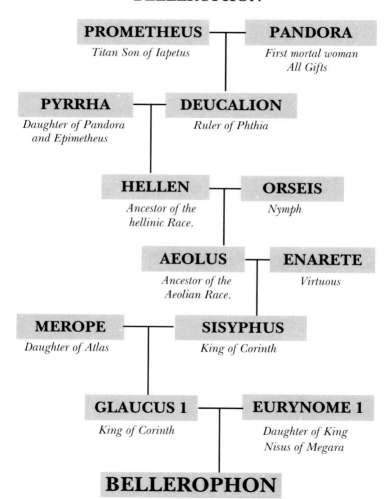

PROMETHEUS
Titan Son of Iapetus

PANDORA
*First mortal woman
All Gifts*

PYRRHA
*Daughter of Pandora
and Epimetheus*

DEUCALION
Ruler of Phthia

HELLEN
*Ancestor of the
hellinic Race.*

ORSEIS
Nymph

AEOLUS
*Ancestor of the
Aeolian Race.*

ENARETE
Virtuous

MEROPE
Daughter of Atlas

SISYPHUS
King of Corinth

GLAUCUS 1
King of Corinth

EURYNOME 1
*Daughter of King
Nisus of Megara*

BELLEROPHON

BELLEROPHON was the son of King GLAUCUS of Corinth, and his mother, on whom ATHENE bestowed the wisdom of the Gods, was EURYNOME 1.*

A somewhat tragic figure, his given name was HIPPONOUS. It was only when he accidentally killed a Corinthian, named Bellerus, that he became known as BELLEROPHON, which translated means Bellerus killer.

He was purified by King PROETUS of Tiryns, whose royal court he joined, but being an extremely handsome young man, he took the eye of the Queen, STHENEBOEA. He did not return her advances, whereupon she informed PROETUS that BELLEROPHON had attempted to seduce her. Now it was a rule of the court that a guest could not be killed, so BELLEROPHON was sent to Lycia, a region in south west Asia Minor, to deliver a message to King IOBATES, the father of STHENEBOEA. BELLEROPHON was unaware that the message requested that he be killed for his supposed violation of the Queen. However, IOBATES had a similar court rule, so to wash his hands of the matter, he gave BELLEROPHON the task of seeking out and killing the CHIMAERA, an offspring of TYPHON and ECHIDNE, a monster with the head of a lion, the tail of a snake and the body of a goat, which breathed great tongues of flame from its mouth.

The CHIMAERA was ravaging the nearby area and IOBATES thought that the task would mean certain death for BELLEROPHON, who agreed to carry it out, so winning the admiration of the Gods. These immortals had already taken an interest in him because several accounts of his birth made his father out to be POSEIDON, who had seduced his mother, EURYNOME. In particular, his guardian Gods were ATHENE and POSEIDON. POSEIDON had produced, from his affair with the dreadful MEDUSA, a remarkable winged horse called

PEGASUS, which constantly rode the skies and was unapproachable.
ATHENE awarded BELLEROPHON a magic, golden bridle and with this he was able to attract PEGASUS, who came to him at the Peirine fountain, in Corinth, allowing him to place the bridle in position. So BELLEROPHON and PEGASUS were united and were to become famous for their exploits.

The Chimaera

Firstly they flew over the CHIMAERA and dropped lead into its mouth. The flames instantly melted the lead which choked the monster to death. IOBATES was amazed with this achievement and asked BELLEROPHON if he could deal with the Solymi, a hostile neighbouring tribe who were threatening Lycia. The Solymi had no answer to the attacks of BELLEROPHON mounted on

PEGASUS and they were firmly routed. Their next target was the Amazons and again the pair prevented any ideas they might have had about invading Lycia.
This seemingly invincible young man perplexed IOBATES, who arranged that his Lycian soldiers should ambush BELLEROPHON. The plan failed and the soldiers were all killed.

It was only at this point that IOBATES realised that BELLEROPHON was guarded and guided by the Gods and his attitude changed completely. He offered the young Hero half of his kingdom and the hand of his daughter, PHILONOE. BELLEROPHON accepted these gifts and remained in Lycia. Some say that he avenged himself on STHENEBOEA by inviting her to ride with him on PEGASUS and, when they were air borne, pushing her off, to her death.

By PHILONOE, BELLEROPHON had two sons and two daughters. He seemed to have the world at his feet. He had the amazing PEGASUS, a loving wife and family and a country whose people adored him.

What caused his tragic end? With all he had, he wanted more, envying the Gods who had adopted him. So he tried to reach Olympus on PEGASUS, but ZEUS sent a gadfly, which stung the winged horse and unseated BELLEROPHON, who fell to earth. He survived the fall but was terribly crippled. His lot was to wander the earth with no comfort or friendship. Homer records 'No one marked the time or place of his death'.

Part 5
JASON

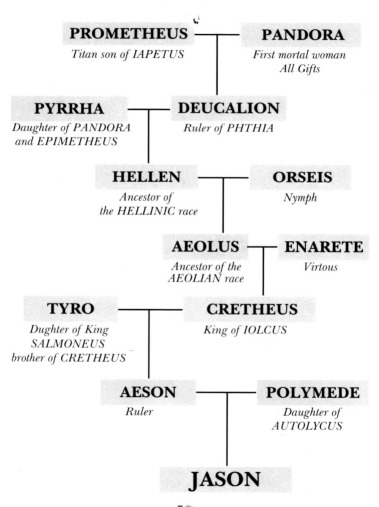

PROMETHEUS
Titan son of IAPETUS

PANDORA
First mortal woman
All Gifts

PYRRHA
Daughter of PANDORA
and EPIMETHEUS

DEUCALION
Ruler of PHTHIA

HELLEN
Ancestor of
the HELLINIC race

ORSEIS
Nymph

AEOLUS
Ancestor of the
AEOLIAN race

ENARETE
Virtous

TYRO
Dughter of King
SALMONEUS
brother of CRETHEUS

CRETHEUS
King of IOLCUS

AESON
Ruler

POLYMEDE
Daughter of
AUTOLYCUS

JASON

JASON was the son of AESON and POLYMEDE. AESON should have succeeded his father to the throne of IOLCUS (present day Volos in Southern Thessaly), but was usurped by his half brother, PELIAS. AESON was persecuted by PELIAS, so when a son DIOMEDES was born to POLYMEDE the baby's safety was paramount. Its parents pretended that the child was dead and then placed it in the care of the wise Centaur, CHEIRON, in his cave on Mount Pelion. CHEIRON, unlike the other Centaurs, was immortal and was directly descended from CRONUS himself. He was both wise and learned and, having re-named the boy JASON, a name which means healed, he reared him including in his education the arts of medicine. CHEIRON provided the same upbringing for other Gods and heroes, including ASCLEPIUS and ACHILLES.

JASON's father, AESON, went in fear of his life, always expecting to be put to death by PELIAS, which led to his eventual suicide. Meanwhile the Delphic oracle predicted that PELIAS would die one day by the hand of a descendant of his grandfather, AEOLUS. So PELIAS set about putting to death every prominent Aeolian he could find. Then a second oracle told him to beware a man wearing only one sandal.

When JASON was twenty years old he set out on a journey to Iolcus, to claim the throne that was rightly his, choosing to arrive at the time when the city paid annual tribute to POSEIDON with a large festival. On his way, he came to the banks of the river Annuras, where an old woman was pleading with passers by to carry her across to the other side. Despite being in a hurry, JASON put her on his back and took her across, but lost one of his sandals in the fast flowing water. There was nothing he could do about it and he did not know that the old woman who had just thanked him was, in fact, the great Goddess HERA, in disguise.

It so happened that HERA had been scorned by PELIAS for many years and she had arrived at that particular time to start a complex chain of events that would give her the revenge she so badly sought and would also conform to the predictions of the two oracles. She chose MEDEA, a sorceress and hand maiden of HECATE, the Goddess of Witchcraft, to play a major role. She needed a reason to bring MEDEA to Iolcus from her home, which at that time was in Colchis, on the far eastern shore of the Black Sea. HERA thought of the Golden Fleece, and decided that if JASON, who she saw as a fine, brave and handsome young man, could be sent to recover the Fleece from Colchis, he would meet MEDEA, claim her as a bride and bring her back to IOLCUS.

Now the Golden Fleece was a ram which had a fleece of gold, could fly and talk and was an offspring of POSEIDON. It came to be in Colchis in the following manner:
King ATHAMUS of Orchomenus had two children, a son PHRIXHUS and a daughter HELLE, by his wife NEPHELE. He then decided to take a second wife, INO, who bore him two more sons. PHRIXHUS was the obvious successor to the throne, which did not please INO, so she devised a wicked plot to clear the way for her own son to succeed. She arranged that the crops would fail by poisoning the seeds and then she reported a false oracle which stated that ATHAMUS needed to sacrifice PHRIXHUS in order to stop the impending famine. Very reluctantly ATHAMUS prepared to sacrifice his son when, out of the skies, sent by ZEUS, came the incredible, flying, golden ram. PHRIXHUS mounted the creature, together with his sister HELLE and they flew away, never to be seen there again. As the ram flew eastwards, HELLE fell into the

sea in a place known today as the Hellespont, but the ram, carrying the boy, continued on its way until they landed at Colchis. PHRIXHUS sacrificed the ram to ZEUS, hanging the Golden Fleece on an oak in the sacred grove of ARES, where it was guarded night and day by an awesome serpent. ZEUS put the image of the ram in the heavens where it is known today as the constellation ARIES.

PHRIXHUS married CHALCIOPE, the daughter of the king of Colchis, had four sons by her, and remained in Colchis for the rest of his life. However, as was the custom, because only women received proper burials in Colchis, PHRIXHUS was denied the ceremony and his spirit was left in turmoil, haunting PELIAS in its great desire to return to its homeland.

The stage was set, the actors in their places and, under the direction of HERA, the action began. In Iolcus, a colleague of PELIAS told him that a stranger had arrived in the city, wearing only one sandal. PELIAS was anxious to see who this might be and sent for the newcomer. When they met, JASON informed him of their relationship and announced that he had come to claim the throne as the eldest son of AESON. Strangely, PELIAS did not argue, but simply said that the throne would be handed over to JASON only after he had freed the country from a curse, which an oracle had stated would be removed when the spirit of PHRIXHUS and the Golden Fleece were returned, in a ship, to their rightful home in Iolcus.

PELIAS said that he would carry out the task himself, but for his advancing years. How could JASON refuse? So began the preparations for a sea journey to Colchis and back. A daunting task that would require skill, determination, courage and strength.

JASON needed a very substantial ship and enlisted the services of the famous shipwright, ARGUS, instructing him to build a fifty oared ship to be called the ARGO.

ARGUS took the best timber from Mount Pelion and ATHENE installed an oracular beam in the prow of the vessel, taken from the prophetic oak tree of ZEUS, in Dodona.

JASON sent messages to all corners of the land, inviting volunteers for the demanding task of crewing the ship and the response included many impressive names, all keen to display their Heroic qualities. HERACLES himself applied, very graciously agreeing to sail under the leadership of JASON. The quest for the Golden Fleece commenced. JASON and his crew set sail from Iolcus, passed Mount Olympus, then turned

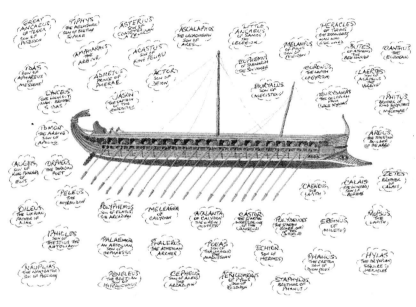

The Argonauts

eastward, making their first port of call the island of Lemnos. At that time, the island was inhabited only by women, as the Goddess APHRODITE had wreaked an odd revenge on the women when they failed to honour her. She made them smell so bad that their husbands stopped having relations with them and took Thracian women as their concubines instead. The women of Lemnos had murdered their husbands as a result and lived alone on the island, freed from the bad odour.

Thinking that the Argonauts, as they were called, were pirates, the women, dressed in their husbands' clothes, rushed to repel the invaders, only to meet ECHION, the first Argonaut ashore. With his charming manner, ECHION satisfied them that he and his companions came in peace and, in order to explain the missing men, HYPSIPYLE, the king's daughter, told him that the women had been cruelly treated by their husbands and had forced the men to emigrate. But now they realized that without men, the Lemnian race would die out. JASON was offered HYPSIPYLE and the throne, if he and his companions would stay. By this time the Argonauts were surrounded by beautiful girls and women, all wanting them to remain. JASON accepted the offer, but said that they would only settle on the island when they had completed their mission for the Golden Fleece. Many children were conceived before the crew left. It was HERACLES who rounded them up and they sailed away reluctantly.

During the night they slipped past the hostile King LAOMEDON of Troy, whose fortress guarded the narrow straits to the Sea of Marmara, known as the Hellespont. Their next stop was Arcton, where they were met by King CYZICUS.

Young king CYZICUS had learned from an oracle that a ship with a band of men would arrive, so he gave them a safe berth and provided them with all their required provisions. He also invited them to his wedding feast, having taken a new bride, CLEITE. During the feast, the Argo was attacked by some six hundred giants, who inhabited the nearby Bear Mountain. They had not reckoned on the guard being HERACLES, whose famous arrows quickly left their dead bodies piled on the beach.

Ironically, when the Argonauts left the hospitable King CYZICUS, the Argo was blown off course during the night and beached. The Argonauts were attacked by a well armed force who obviously took them for pirates and following an intense battle, many dead lay at their feet, one of them being no other than CYZICUS himself, the Argo having been blown back to another part of Arcton. Poor CLEITE hanged herself when she heard the news.

The Argo continued on its way and a contest was held, to see who could row for the longest time. The victor, as expected, was HERACLES, but he broke his oar, which caused a stop, when he went in search of suitable wood with which to fashion a new one. Now HERACLES' young companion of the voyage was a handsome lad called HYLAS. HERACLES had been responsible for killing the boy's father in a dispute and so had taken the youngster under his wing. Young HYLAS had gone to fetch drinking water and when he failed to return, HERACLES and POLYPHEMUS went to search for the boy. HYLAS' voice was heard crying for help, but he could not be found, the reason being that he had been abducted to the underwater grotto of the nymph DRYOPE and her sisters, who had been captivated by the boy's beauty. HERACLES was distraught and they continued the search for so long that the Argo, having found a good wind, set sail without them, at the insistence of CALAIS and ZETES, the winged sons of BOREAS, the North Wind. HERACLES never forgot this desertion and it is said that many years later, he killed both CALAIS and ZETES on the island of Tenos.

The Argonauts next port of call was Bebyros, which was ruled by King AMYCUS, a famed boxer who challenged strangers to fight, killing them if they accepted and killing them if they refused. AMYCUS refused to provision the Argo unless one of the crew fought him. Having lost HERACLES, who would have been the obvious choice, the Argonauts put forward POLYDEUCES, also known as POLLUX, a twin with CASTOR of the famous DIOSCURI. He had won a boxing contest at the Olympic Games and was a formidable contestant. AMYCUS found out just how good POLYDEUCES was, when he was fatally defeated in a fierce fight.

The Argo next reached Salmydessus, in eastern Thrace, where PHINEUS reigned; an accomplished prophet who had been punished by the Gods. They had blinded him and plagued his everyday life by sending the HARPIES to torment him. When PHINEUS invited the Argonauts to his table, they repaid his hospitality by driving away the HARPIES with the aid of the airborne CALAIS and ZETES, who chased them with brandished swords. The grateful prophet, PHINEUS, taught JASON the intricate navigation that he would need if the Argo was to negotiate the hazards of the Bosphorus, the entrance to the Black Sea. PHINEAS also forecast their fortune on the forthcoming journey, including weather and hospitality, ending with the words: 'When you reach Colchis, trust in APHRODITE'.

The first hazard, at the entrance to the Bosphorus, was a group of rocks known as the Sympleglades. These rocks were able to change their position and were known to perform a pincer movement, crushing any passing ship. (A modern explanation of these moving rocks is that at certain times of the year, icefloes come into the Black Sea from the Russian rivers.)
Following the advice of PHINEUS and timing the movements of the rocks, the Argonauts quickly rowed through with only minor damage to the stern of the ship.

At the island of Thymias, APOLLO appeared to them and

ORPHEUS, the Thracian poet and a crew member, sacrificed a wild goat to the God. APOLLO made the Argonauts swear to be loyal to each other under all circumstances.

Reaching the city of Mariandyne, they had the ill luck to lose two of the crew when IDMON was badly gashed by a wild boar and bled to death, while the helmsman, TIPHYS, took sick and died. ANCAEUS was then chosen to steer the Argo and at the next stop, Sinope, JASON was able to recruit three more crew, namely the brothers DEILON, AUTOLYCUS and PHLOGIUS. These three had fought with HERACLES against the AMAZONS and they had been stranded at Sinope ever since.

On sailed the Argo, past the land of the AMAZONS and the country of Chalybia, where the Chalybians were noted for their skill in forging iron. Past the land of the Tibarenians, whose custom was for the men to groan with the pains of childbirth when their wives were in labour, and sailing along the coastline of the Moesynoechians, a race who were sexually promiscuous, lived in wooden castles and carried long spears with ivy shaped shields. Strange lands and people with even stranger customs were certainly adding adventure to this remarkable expedition.

Near the island of ARES they were attacked by the Stymphalian birds with their brazen plumage, who lived in the area following their removal from Lake Stymphalia, in Arcadia, by HERACLES, during his sixth labour. On the advice of PHINEUS, the Argonauts donned their headgear and clashed their swords against their shields, the terrible din frightening the birds away. PHINEUS had told them to

stop at this island and the reason became clear when four men, the sons of PHRIXHUS and CHALCIOPE, were washed up on the shore after being shipwrecked. They were made very welcome and they joined the depleted crew. On they sailed, past the island of Philyra, the birth place of the wise Centaur CHEIRON, whose mother PHILYRA had been seduced by CRONUS. The God had disguised himself as a horse in order to avoid detection by his wife, RHEA. The result of the union was half man, half horse, a Centaur.

The Argonauts now reached the Caucasus mountains and entered the river Phasis, whose waters irrigated the Colchis area. JASON concealed the Argo, at this point, in a back water and summoned a meeting to discuss their plan of attack.
HERA and ATHENE, who had been watching and guiding the Argo all along, now contacted APHDRODITE, whose companion EROS was needed to instill the attraction called love into the hearts of JASON and MEDEA, such that when they met, they would be overwhelmed with the need for each other.
At JASON's meeting, it was decided that he should take the four sons of PHRIXUS and also AUGEIS, who was the half brother of King AEETES of Colchis, to ask the king for permission to take back the Golden Fleece. On their way, the group met CHALCIOPE, who was surprised to see her sons and, on learning the story of their survival, thanked JASON profusely. On meeting AEETES, it was left to AUGEIS to explain their mission.

AEETES was furious and was ordering them to leave or face punishment, when MEDEA appeared and had a calming influence on her father. He agreed to give JASON the fleece, but only on the successful completion of a task.

JASON was to yoke two fire-breathing bulls, which had feet of bronze fashioned by the God HEPHAESTUS. He was then to use them to plough the field of ARES, after which he had to sow the ground with serpents' teeth. It was at that

moment that EROS fired his arrow into the heart of
MEDEA and she was overwhelmed with love for JASON.
MEDEA agreed to help the Hero with his task, provided
that he would make her his wife and take her back with him
in the Argo. JASON swore to love MEDEA for eternity, an
oath he made to all the Olympian gods.

MEDEA gave JASON the red juice of the Caucasian crocus,
a lotion that would protect him from the fiery breath of the
bulls. JASON painted the juice on his body and armament
and was then able to handle the animals, which he
harnessed to a plough. All day he ploughed and then
planted the serpents' teeth, which at once sprouted into
armed warriors. JASON provoked and taunted the troops
to turn one upon the other, which they did with great
ferocity, until none remained.
However, AEETES did not keep his word and refused to
give JASON the Fleece. In fact he threatened JASON and
his companions with death unless they left empty-handed.

It was MEDEA who again came to the rescue, with a plan.
She led JASON and some of the Argonauts to the grove of
ARES, where the Golden Fleece was hanging under the
watchful eye of the immortal dragon, which had a thousand
coils and was of immense size, some say as large as the Argo
itself. MEDEA worked her magic when she put the serpent
into a trance with incantations and droplets of juniper,
sprinkling the latter on its eyelids.
JASON took the Fleece quickly and they hurried to the
place where the Argo lay. The priestesses of ARES raised
the alarm and the Argo was attacked by the Colchians.
There were many injuries, but the Argonauts made good
their escape. MEDEA healed all but one of the injured; only
IPHITUS was a fatal casualty.
Various stories exist, of the different routes taken by the
Argo on her homeward journey, most of them discounted
in the light of the present geographical knowledge of Asia

Minor and Europe. It is therefore safer to assume that the Argonauts returned by the same route as they had travelled on the outward journey, via the Bosphorus. The Hellespont, by that time no longer dominated by Troy, which had been captured by HERACLES, would pose no problem.

The Argo, however, was pursued on its way by the Colchians, led by APSYRTUS, the young half brother of MEDEA, who was tricked by her into thinking that she had been abducted against her will and wanted to return to Colchis. When APSYRTUS came for her, JASON was in hiding and he struck the Colchian a fatal blow from behind. JASON then carried out a ritual with the blood of APSYRTUS, to prevent the young man's ghost from haunting him.

The Colchians continued to chase the Argo, with strict instructions to bring back both MEDEA and the Golden Fleece. They eventually caught up with the Argonauts at Corcyra (today known as Kerkira or Corfu), where the island was reigned by King ALCINOUS and Queen ARETE. They demanded, in the name of King AEETES, that ALCINOUS give them MEDEA and the Fleece, and ALCINOUS would have been obliged to have done so, within the bounds of royal protocol, had it not been for MEDEA, who appealed to Queen ARETE for protection. She asked the queen to keep her husband awake all night by pleading and listing to him all the cases in which daughters had been ill treated by their fathers. The tired king gave way and simply decreed that if MEDEA was a virgin, she should return to Colchis and, if not, she was at liberty to stay, along with JASON.

JASON was advised to act with haste and, that same day, he married MEDEA in the Cave of Macris. The marriage was consummated following a wedding feast, when the Golden Fleece was laid upon the marriage bed.

The Colchians, afraid of their fate, should they return to AEETES empty handed, decided to stay and they settled in Corcyra.

The Argo, which had gone wildly off course in reaching Corcyra, now needed to retrace its path around the Peloponnese and head north to Iolcus, with the Fleece. The journey was far from over, because violent storms and high winds took them via Sicily and Libya. It was off the coast of Libya that a massive tidal wave threw the ship several miles inland, stranding the Argonauts in the desert. In JASON's sleep he was told where to find drinking water for himself and his companions and advised of the actions necessary to return the Argo to the sea. It was here that they lost CANTHUS when he was killed by a Libyan shepherd, also MOPSUS, who was bitten in the heel by a serpent and who died an agonizing death. They paid tribute to the God TRITON with the sacrifice of a sheep. TRITON gave EUPHEMUS the sovereign rights to the region and the God physically pulled the Argo to the Mediterranean coast. Reaching Crete, the Argonauts were attacked by a bronze sentinel called TALOS, who used large rocks as his ammunition. It was MEDEA with her magic potions who induced sleep before removing a bronze nail from the neck of TALOS, thus draining the body of its life giving ichor.

The Argo arrived at Aegina, where the crew had some light relief, taking part in a contest which entailed taking a pitcher to a watering place, filling it and returning to the ship, a race which is still an annual custom on the island.

The remainder of the Argonauts' journey went smoothly, until at last they reached the beach of Pagasae, near Iolcus. It was here that JASON heard of the death of his mother, POLYMEDE, who had committed suicide under the stress from the cruelty inflicted on her by PELIAS. Of course,

PELIAS had never expected the Argo to return and, totally unaware of the success of the Argonauts' mission, was continuing with his wicked regime.

JASON met with his companions to discuss how they could best take Iolcus and rid the region of PELIAS for ever. They thought of each returning to their home towns, to raise as many men as possible, in order to form an army large enough to take the well fortified Iolcus, but again it was MEDEA who told them that she could take the city on her own, if they would just follow her instructions.
The Argonauts were to hide the Argo on a secluded and heavily wooded beach, within sight of Iolcus. When they saw a waving light from the palace roof, it would mean that PELIAS was dead and the city gates open.

In the meantime, that night, MEDEA, together with her twelve handmaidens, made their way towards Iolcus. Carrying an image of the Goddess ARTEMIS and dressed in strange gowns, they looked a wierd party, led by MEDEA, who had taken on the appearance of an old hag. The sentinels had no option but to admit the group to the city, when MEDEA announced that they had been sent to give the news that ARTEMIS intended to heap good fortune on Iolcus.
Once inside, MEDEA and her handmaidens raged through the city in the manner of the famous Bacchantes (the female votaries of DIONYSUS, who partook in orgiastic rites, working themselves and their audience into a wild frenzy), awakening the inhabitants and inducing a religious hysteria. PELIAS himself woke and in a bewildered state, asked MEDEA what the strange intrusion meant. MEDEA told him that ARTEMIS had seen fit to befriend Iolcus and that the Goddess would rejuvenate PELIAS, to allow him to produce an heir to his throne. (You will see on the crew list,

that the king's son, ACASTUS, had given his service to JASON, on the Argo.)

The king was dubious of the claims made by MEDEA, who responded by magically returning to her youthful state before his eyes, explaining the transition by exclaiming: 'Such is the power of ARTEMIS!' MEDEA then took an old ram, cut it into many pieces and boiled it in a cauldron. With incantations, MEDEA wove her spell, all the time imploring ARTEMIS to help her, at the crucial moment, with sleight of hand, producing a baby lamb from the wooden image of ARTEMIS. PELIAS was then convinced and MEDEA charmed him to sleep.

These events were witnessed by the three daughters of PELIAS, and MEDEA instructed them to cut up their father and place the pieces in the cauldron, just as they had seen the ram treated. While one daughter refused, the others agreed and set about their grisly task with enthusiasm. MEDEA then told them to take the cauldron to the palace roof, each carrying a torch, and there to bring the cauldron to the boil, whilst invoking the moon.

The Argonauts saw the lights, knew that MEDEA had been successful and entered the city without resistance. JASON gave the throne to ACASTUS (some say that he was exiled with MEDEA for the murder of PELIAS), rather than remain as king himself, especially as he hoped to eventually inherit the throne of Corinth, his wife MEDEA being next in line for this royal seat, following the death of King CORINTHUS.

First, however, JASON went to Orchomenus, where the Golden Fleece was placed in the temple of ZEUS. He then beached the Argo at Corinth and dedicated the ship to POSEIDON. MEDEA claimed the throne and JASON reigned happily with her for ten years, during which time they had two sons, MERMERUS and PHERES.

It is said that JASON had come to suspect that MEDEA had poisoned CORINTHUS in order to succeed to the throne and intended to divorce her after his successful approach to King CREON of Thebes for the hand of his daughter GLAUCE in marriage. MEDEA reminded JASON of the oath he had made to all the Olympian Gods, to remain always faithful to her. She also reminded him that it was she who had put him on the throne of Corinth, but her pleas were to no avail. JASON went ahead with the divorce and married GLAUCE, underestimating the terrible revenge of MEDEA, who used fire to murder GLAUCE, her father King CREON and all the royal guests, when at the wedding feast the palace was set alight by MEDEA's gift to GLAUCE. This was a golden crown and a white robe which Medea ignited by magic. Only JASON escaped the holocaust that followed, by jumping clear, through a palace window. MEDEA had not finished, as she next committed the heinous crime of sacrificing her two sons on the altar of the temple of HERA, encouraged by that Goddess, who promised to make them immortal.

What a tragic end for JASON and his illustrious career. It is said that he roamed the land, despised by all, who blamed him for the terrible vengeance of MEDEA. The Gods had deserted him and in his old age he returned to Corinth where he sat, amongst his memories, under the beached Argo. He thought of hanging himself from the prow, but, as if the ship knew, before he made a move, it suddenly toppled over, crushing him to death.

To end this tale of the adventures of this Heroic band of men, it is of interest to recount one short story concerning the helmsman of the Argo, one ANCAEUS. He returned, at the end of the voyage, to his palace in Tegrea. It had been prophesied, before he left, that he would never again taste the wine from his own vineyard.

On his arrival, he was met by his steward, who informed him that the grapes had been harvested and a jug of the first wine awaited him. ANCAEUS, recalling the prophecy, ridiculed his seer for its falseness and was just about to take his first swallow when the prophet uttered a warning. All at once, great cries were heard outside. On inquiry, ANCAEUS was told that a wild boar was ravaging the vineyards. Putting down his cup, he took up his spear and went out to deal with the wild intruder. The animal surprised him from its hiding place behind a bush and gored him to death. The seer's warning words? He had said:

'Sire, there is many a slip 'twixt cup and lip', and thus the proverb was born.

Part 6
ACHILLES

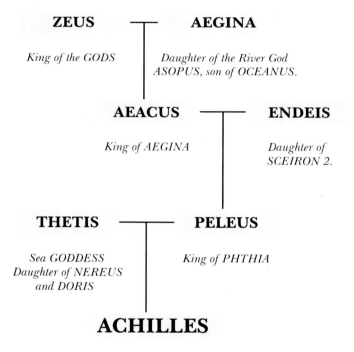

ZEUS ———— AEGINA

King of the GODS   *Daughter of the River God*
                          ASOPUS, son of OCEANUS.

AEACUS ———— ENDEIS

King of AEGINA   *Daughter of*
                         SCEIRON 2.

THETIS ———— PELEUS

Sea GODDESS   *King of PHTHIA*
Daughter of NEREUS
and DORIS

ACHILLES

A son was born to PELEUS, the king of Phthia, and THETIS, a sea Goddess. They called him LIGYRON and THETIS wished to make the child immortal. Some say that she attempted to do this in the traditional manner, by bathing the baby in ambrosia by day and laying it in the dying embers of the fire at night, an act which so alarmed PELEUS that she pulled the child from the fire by his right ankle. Others say that

THETIS took the child to the immortal river STYX, to give the baby immortality by totally immersing him in the river, holding him by the right ankle as she dipped him into the waters. Either way, the fact remains that LIGYRON was immortal, apart from the ankle and heel of his right foot.

THETIS deserted PELEUS and the child, returning to the watery depths; so PELEUS took the baby to the wise Centaur, CHEIRON, who reared the child in a most natural way, whilst providing an education which included singing, hunting and healing. CHEIRON re-named the child ACHILLES and, as we shall learn later in this account, the saying was born (in common use today) whereby, when describing any person's weak spot, we call it their 'ACHILLES heel'.

ACHILLES grew to become handsome, courageous and fleet of foot. It is reported that, when he was only six years, he killed his first wild boar and that he could run as fast as the stags which he hunted. His reputation spread so that no gathering of Heroes would have been complete without him.

ACHILLES' mother, THETIS, had always kept a watchful eye on his development, knowing that, should he ever join a Heroes' expedition, he would gain fame and glory, but he would not return. On the other hand, if he stayed at home, he would live a long but undistinguished life.

Now recruits were being sought for an armed force to sail to Troy, where HELEN, wife of MENELAUS, had been abducted to that city by PARIS, thus giving rise to the expedition formed to rescue her and punish the Trojan effrontery. A prophecy had stated that Troy could never be taken without the help of ACHILLES; so ODYSSEUS, NESTOR and AJAX were sent to SCYROS, to fetch the young boy (ACHILLES was only fifteen at the time) from the court of King LYCOMEDES, where rumour had it that he had been hidden by his mother for safekeeping, in the guise of a girl.

In order to find ACHILLES, ODYSSEUS laid out all manner of gifts for the girls of the court, including a shield and a spear, inviting them to take their pick. As they were doing so, ODYSSEUS ordered a commotion outside, accompanied by warlike blasts of the trumpet. Immediately, one of the 'girls' stripped to the waist, grabbed the shield and spear and rushed outside. ACHILLES' disguise had been discovered and he then agreed to lead a force of Myrmidons, a tribe from southern Thessaly, to Troy. He was made Admiral of the Greek Fleet with the blessing of his father, PELEUS and, when PHOENIX, the king of the Dolopians, offered his services as the boy's guardian, the young ACHILLES was ready for action; he also had his cousin, PATROCLUS, with him and they were to become inseparable companions. The Greek Fleet was assembled at Aulis, a force of several hundred ships.

At this point we should mention the leading personages in what was to become the famous Siege of Troy. Whilst ACHILLES commanded the Hellenic Fleet, with PHOENIX and GREAT AJAX as his immediate aides, it was AGAMEMNON, king of Mycenae and brother of MENELAUS, who commanded the Hellenic Army on board, with ODYSSEUS, PALAMEDES and DIOMEDES as his chief officers, together with the wise king, NESTOR, as his most influential advisor.

GREAT AJAX was a remarkable young man, coming second only to ACHILLES in strength, courage and good looks. A huge man, whom HERACLES had made invulnerable apart from his armpit and neck, he carried a massive shield, fashioned from the hides of seven bulls. The son of TELAMON, king of Salamis, he was advised by his father to always seek the assistance of the Gods in battle, but the confident young Hero was, on many occasions, to remark that he needed help from no one and it is said that he incurred much divine wrath.

GREAT AJAX had a half brother, TEUCER, reputed to be the best archer in Greece, who fought from behind the shelter of the great shield which GREAT AJAX carried. So they always fought together, along with LITTLE AJAX, who, whilst no relation to GREAT AJAX, was the undoubted champion spear thrower of all Greece and though small in stature, was second only to ACHILLES in fleetness of foot.

As for ODYSSEUS, whose name means 'the angry one', this remarkable Hero is covered in some detail in a later chapter. While he served alongside his fellow officer, PALAMEDES, he suffered from an intense hatred of this man, because it had been a clever ruse of PALAMEDES which had engineered his enlistment for the expedition to Troy.
PALAMEDES was the son of NAUPLIAS and CLYMENE 2* and, some say, it was he who invented many letters of the alphabet.
DIOMEDES was the son of TYDEUS, noted as one of the famous 'Seven against Thebes'. DIOMEDES himself became an impressive Argive leader, avenging his father's death when, with other sons of the Seven, they razed Thebes to the ground. He was a fearless warrior and became almost inseparable from ODYSSEUS in thier battlefield exploits at Troy.

ACHILLES and his Fleet sailed for Troy, but a mixture of poor navigation, with severe weather sent by the ever vengeful HERA, drove them to the island of Mysia, which they began to ravage, believing that they had arrived at Troy.

Now ACHILLES had been given a famous spear, which only he could wield. It had originally been a present from the Centaur, CHEIRON, to his father, PELEUS, before being passed down to ACHILLES.

A battle raged on Mysia, and ACHILLES and his men were driven back to their ships by TELEPHUS, the king of the island, and his troops. TELEPHUS himself was confronted by ACHILLES and PATROCLUS, and whilst running away, he tripped over a vine root and was speared in the thigh by ACHILLES and his powerful weapon. Some say that the root was placed in his path by DIONYSUS, the God of Wine, whom TELEPHUS had failed to honour. The Greek ships returned home, and it was to be a considerable time before they would re-assemble for a second attempt to storm Troy.

In the meantime, an oracle had stated that they would never reach Troy without the guidance of TELEPHUS, but he was dying from the festering wounds inflicted by the spear of ACHILLES. APOLLO was consulted and he gave the oracle-like advice which stated that the wounds of TELEPHUS could only be healed by their cause. TELEPHUS went to Mycenae in disguise and begged AGAMEMNON's help. AGAMEMNON interpreted the advice of APOLLO, deciding that the cause was the spear of ACHILLES and, when rust was scraped from it and applied to the wound, a miraculous cure took place. The efficacy of this treatment is born out by the ancient homoeopathic principle that like cures like.

The Fleet gathered once more at Aulis, as King PRIAM of Troy was still adamant that there would be no returning HELEN. King PRIAM sent his priest, CALCHAS, to consult

the Delphic oracle. The priest was told that
Troy would be defeated and that he himself
should join the Greek forces. So CALCHAS
swore an oath of allegiance to ACHILLES
in the forthcoming venture and the Fleet
set sail.

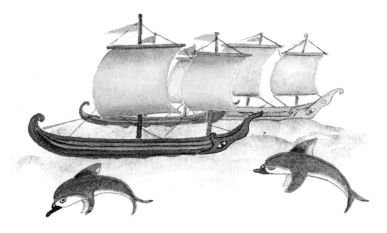

The Fleet at Aulis

There seems to have been very little
compassion in the make up of ACHILLES.
He was a ruthless fighter and often failed to
take the sound advice of his mother,
THETIS. She warned him that if he ever
killed a son of APOLLO, then he himself
would die at the hand of the god. In fact,
ACHILLES had a servant with him, called
MNEMON, whose duty it was to remind
him constantly of this prediction.

When the Fleet reached the island of
Tenedos, which was in sight of Troy, the
expedition was attacked by the young king

of the island, named TENES, thought to be the son of CYCNUS and PROCLEIA, but actually he had been born from his mother's union with APOLLO. TENES hurled rocks at the Greek ships and ACHILLES, without thinking, swam ashore and pierced him through the heart with his sword. The army landed and ravaged the island.

It was then that ACHILLES learned that TENES was descended from APOLLO and in a rage he killed poor MNEMON for failing to warn him. The father of TENES was CYCNUS 3*, king of Colonae, near Troy and himself a son of POSEIDON. King CYCNUS the Third took part in the first attempt to repulse the Greek landing on Troy, only to die at the hands of ACHILLES, who strangled him with the thongs of his helmet, having found that POSEIDON had made his son invulnerable to weapons. It is said that POSEIDON turned his dead son into a swan, 'cycnus' being the name for this bird.

Another warning to ACHILLES from his mother stated that the first man to land would be the first to die and this time he heeded the warning. The first man on to Trojan soil was PROTESILAUS who, after killing several Trojans, was killed by HECTOR, the son of King PRIAM.

There is a story that says that the brave PROTESILAUS was so badly missed by his wife when he left with the Fleet, that she made a waxen image of him and laid it in their marriage bed. When she learned of his death, she begged ZEUS to give her just three more hours with her husband. ZEUS consented and returned the spirit of PROTESILAUS, from Tartarus, to give life to the wax image. Following three hours of love, PROTESILAUS begged his wife to follow him as soon as possible; so while she was still in his arms, she took a knife and killed herself.

An oracle had stated that Troy would not fall if King

PRIAM's son, TROILUS, should reach the age of twenty. It is said that, whilst engaged in combat with this beautiful young boy, ACHILLES actually fell in love with him, even to the point of saying

'I will kill you unless you yield to my caresses'.

TROILUS ran away and took refuge in the temple to APOLLO, but ACHILLES found him and beheaded the youth on the altar. Ironically, this was the very place where ACHILLES would eventually meet his death.

The Trojan war lasted for ten years and during the first nine, it was important to stop supplies from reaching Troy via the many regions and cities in that part of the world, which were loyal to King PRIAM.

ACHILLES took charge of both naval and land forces and one by one he conquered and sacked the various sources of supply. Twelve cities were taken from the sea and a further eleven fell in land battles. These actions were a double edged sword because, whilst they prevented food and provisions from reaching Troy, at the same time they provided all the requirements for the Greek army.

The raids also provided a stream of concubines for the Greek warriors, thus maintaining a high morale among the troops. However, these abductions were a source of trouble occasionally. ACHILLES had selected a woman for himself, a certain BRISEIS, but AGAMEMNON took a fancy to her and stole her from our Hero, so causing a split in the Greek unity. ACHILLES refused to partake further in the war and the remaining forces, under AGAMEMNON, suffered several humiliating defeats. In despair, AGAMEMNON gave in, sending ODYSSEUS, GREAT AJAX and PHOENIX to see ACHILLES, sending many gifts, promising to return BRISEIS and pleading with the Hero to return to the war.

Despite all this, ACHILLES would not change his position and told the envoys that he intended to return to Greece the next day. However, that very day, an incident occurred that caused him to change his mind.

His dearest friend, PATROCLUS, wearing ACHILLES' armour, repelled a Trojan attack on the ship, and then drove on relentlessly almost to the city walls. It required the intervention of APOLLO himself to push PATROCLUS to the ground and disarm him, allowing HECTOR to kill the valiant Hero with ease. ACHILLES was enraged and swore vengeance on Troy and on HECTOR in particular. It was this cruel loss of his dear friend that made ACHILLES join the battle once more. Never had he felt so much grief and it is said that he rolled in the dust and wept.

ACHILLES made peace with AGAMEMNON, who returned BRISEIS to him, assuring him that she had only been taken in anger, not in lust.

Donning a new suit of armour provided by HEPHAESTUS and delivered by his mother, bent on revenge for the death of his soulmate, ACHILLES was now in an angry mood which spelled trouble for the Trojans. Killing all before him, he finally cornered HECTOR, who tried to out run ACHILLES, but was unable to reach the safety of the city.

Fighting stopped and the warriors of both sides became spectators to the clash between ACHILLES and HECTOR. However, the fight did not last long, as ACHILLES ran his sword through the chest of HECTOR, before dragging the dead body around the city walls, behind his chariot, for all Troy to witness.

ACHILLES came to bury PATROCLUS with some feeling of satisfaction, but he marked the ceremony by sacrificing further sons of PRIAM, plus twelve Trojan prisoners, slitting their throats before heaping them on the funeral pyre, which was fuelled with the very best timber. Funeral games were held in honour of PATROCLUS. The wrestling match resulted in a tie between GREAT AJAX and ODYSSEUS, while DIOMEDES won the chariot race. For some time afterwards, ACHILLES performed the daily task of dragging HECTOR's body around the tomb of PATROCLUS and it needed a visit from HERMES, on the instructions of ZEUS, to persuade the Hero to accept a ransom from PRIAM, who desperately wanted the mutilated body of his son, for proper burial. ACHILLES demanded payment in gold equal to the weight of HECTOR's body and huge scales were erected, to take HECTOR on one side, while all the available gold in Troy was heaped on the other side.

One of Troy's fiercest fighters was the Amazon queen, PENTHESILEIA, who won the respect of ACHILLES for her courage in the field. Eventually she died by the sword of ACHILLES and it is said that, falling in love with her dead body, he decided to bury her with honour. This led to insolent remarks from the Greek warrior, THERSITES, cousin of DIOMEDES. ACHILLES reacted by smashing his head, killing him. DIOMEDES then opposed ACHILLES, but ODYSSEUS, who had been a staunch companion of DIOMEDES, sided with ACHILLES and even purified him of the killing.

PRIAM received great help from his half brother, TITHONUS, governor of Assyria, who sent his son, MEMNON (known as the Ethiopian), to Troy, with more than two thousand men and chariots. MEMNON was a handsome black prince with a reputation for skill and courage on the battle field. He killed many Greeks, the most notable being ANTILOCHUS, the young son of NESTOR. The lad had only recently joined the expedition and when ACHILLES heard the news, he hurried to the scene, having a particularly high regard for the young

Hero, where he found MEMNON in direct combat with GREAT AJAX. ACHILLES brushed GREAT AJAX aside and, taking his place, soon dealt a death blow to MEMNON, whose head and armour were thrown on the funeral pyre of ANTILOCHUS.

The Trojans were close to defeat when APOLLO and POSEIDON decided to exact their revenge for the deaths of their sons, TROILUS and CYCNUS. The prophecy of THETIS came true, as in the midst of yet another battle, APOLLO found PARIS and led him to the temple of APOLLO, where ACHILLES was fighting, and, guiding the Trojan's arrows, shot him in the one mortal spot on his body, the right heel. ACHILLES died an agonizing death and his brave friend, GREAT AJAX carried his body back to the Greek encampment.

The ghosts of ACHILLES, PATROCLUS and ANTILOCHUS are said to be found in the asphodel fields of Elysium, the underworld dwelling place of mortals who the Gods have chosen to make immortal.

Part 7

ODYSSEUS

PROMETHEUS ——— **PANDORA**

TITAN son of IAPETUS

First mortal woman
(All Gifts)

PYRRHA ——— **DEUCALION**

Daughter of PANDORA
and EPIMETHEUS

Ruler of PHTHIA

HELLEN ——— **ORSEIS**

Ancestor of the Hellinic race

Nymph

AEOLUS ——— **ENARETE**

Ancestor of the
Aeolian Race

Virtuous

ANTICLEIA ——— **SISYPHUS**

Daughter of AUTOLYCUS,
wife of King LAERTES
of ITHACA.

King of CORINTH

ODYSSEUS

This renowned Hero was brought up as the son of King LAERTES of Ithaca and ANTICLEIA, daughter of AUTOLYCUS. In actual fact, his father was SISYPHUS, as he was conceived from an adulterous affair.

With a heritage that included the blood of both AUTOLYCUS and SISYPHUS, ODYSSEUS was surely endowed with a generous supply of thievery, trickery and general roguery, for those two old scoundrels were famous for these characteristics, which were often to stand ODYSSEUS in good stead in his numerous predicaments.

Like almost every other young prince in Greece, ODYSSEUS sought the hand of the beautiful HELEN, daughter of TYNDAREUS, king of Sparta, but he also guessed that she was likely to choose the very wealthy MENELAUS.

Now TYNDAREUS was worried at the consequences of HELEN having so many suitors, because there was bound to be much jealousy, which could lead to violence. The wily ODYSSEUS told TYNDAREUS that he would solve this problem, if the king could influence his brother, ICARIUS, to give him the hand of his daughter, PENELOPE, in marriage.

It was agreed. ODYSSEUS then told TYNDAREUS to make all the suitors of HELEN swear on oath, that they would defend her chosen husband against any future problems arising from the marriage. ODYSSEUS himself was the first to take the vow of allegiance. PENELOPE became his bride and, despite her father's wishes that they remain in Lacedaemonia, (the ancient name for Sparta) they returned to live in Ithaca.

Not long afterwards, HELEN married MENELAUS, as ODYSSEUS had predicted, but he had not expected his advice to TYNDAREUS to be executed so soon, for HELEN eloped with PARIS, son of King PRIAM of Troy, and MENELAUS turned to his brother, AGAMEMNON, for help. Recruitment for an expedition to Troy began by enforcing the oath made by all the princes who had sought HELEN's hand.

MENELAUS, accompanied by PALAMEDES, paid a visit to each prince in turn, but ODYSSEUS, who wanted to avoid recruitment, heard of the deputation and feigned madness as an excuse for being an unsuitable candidate. He was found by the conscriptors, ploughing a field with a mixture of horse and ox in the yoke and sprinkling the ground with salt. The shrewd PALAMEDES guessed that it was a trick, so he snatched the baby TELEMACHUS, the son of ODYSSEUS and PENELOPE, from its mother's arms and laid it on the ground in the direct path of the plough. ODYSSEUS immediately took action to avoid trampling the baby, thus showing that he was perfectly sane.

ODYSSEUS had no option but to honour his pledge, but he was never to forgive PALAMEDES, to whom he became a life-long enemy. This was ironic however, because, as you will read elsewhere, ODYSSEUS showed just as much cunning, when he tricked the young ACHILLES into going to Troy, when the boy had been disguised as a girl to avoid conscription.

Despite the initial reluctance of ODYSSEUS, he was nevertheless to become one of the greatest Heroes of the Trojan war, a campaign that was to occupy a long and eventful period in his life.

He commanded twelve ships which he gathered from Ithaca, Cephallenia and Zacynthus, and he was employed by AGAMEMNON and ACHILLES on many occasions when they needed a diplomat, because, besides his cunning nature, he also had a very persuasive tongue. His feats on the battle field were surpassed only by ACHILLES and possibly GREAT AJAX.

When ACHILLES was killed, it was GREAT AJAX who carried the body back to camp while ODYSSEUS fought a rearguard action that gave GREAT AJAX safe passage. This incident ended tragically, however, because both Heroes claimed the weaponry of ACHILLES. It took a court decision to award the armament to ODYSSEUS, whereupon the distraught AJAX went mad and committed suicide.

It was ODYSSEUS who discovered the three oracles which aided the defeat of Troy, following the death of ACHILLES. They were:
1) NEOPTOLEMUS, a son of ACHILLES, needed to be recruited by the Greek Forces.
2) PHILOCTETES, owner of the famous bow and arrows of HERACLES, should be brought to Troy.
3) The Palladium, an ancient statue of ATHENE, had to be stolen from the Pergamum, the Trojan citadel.
ODYSSEUS fulfilled the requirements of all three oracles when he firstly located and recruited NEOPTOLEMUS, giving the young man the armaments of his father, ACHILLES. Secondly he travelled with DIOMEDES to Lemnos, where, with the help of HERACLES, they brought PHILOCTETES to Troy. Then, again with DIOMEDES, he succeeded in stealing the Palladium.

ODYSSEUS' paramount claim to fame was the formulation of the plan involving the wooden horse, which was to become the means of obtaining entry into Troy, thus bringing about the fall of the city and the end of the bitter struggle that had raged for ten years.
The idea was blessed by ATHENE and HERMES, the Goddess supervising the building of the immense structure,

which was erected by EPEIUS, a Phocian from Parnassus. EPEIUS had been born a coward, in atonement for his father's false vows to ATHENE, although he was a skilled artisan and a clever boxer. The huge wooden horse was hollow, having a trapdoor in its flank, with a rope ladder to allow access. The plan was to load the horse with warriors and, whilst there are differing reports as to actual numbers, it is probable that fifty was nearest the mark.

ODYSSEUS, seconded by DIOMEDES, was to lead the expedition and, unwillingly, the last man to board was EPEIUS, who knew the workings of the trap door. Carved on the side of the horse was a tribute to ATHENE and when it was complete and full, the huge structure was left standing on the beach.

That night, AGAMEMNON and the remainder of the Greek force extinguished their fires, broke camp, boarded their ships and withdrew to the nearby island of Tenedos. The next morning, the Trojans discovered the scene, deserted but for the large wooden horse. They were puzzled as to its meaning, until PRIAM's son, THYMOETES, said that as, from the inscription, it was clearly a gift to ATHENE, they should haul it to her temple in the city and dedicate it to her. There were mixed feelings, but PRIAM supported his son's idea and with much difficulty, the horse was transported to the temple within the city.

CASSANDRA, the daughter of PRIAM, was convinced that the horse contained armed men. She was supported by LAOCOON, a Trojan priest, who cried;

'You fools! Never trust a Greek, even if he brings you gifts.'

With that, he hurled a spear at the horse and a noise of clashing weapons was heard from within the frame of the giant structure.

The situation was saved by the arrival of some Trojan

guards who had a Greek prisoner called SINON with them. PRIAM questioned SINON, who explained that he had escaped as the Greek fleet set sail, because he was being falsely tried for a crime that had been committed by ODYSSEUS. He told PRIAM that the Greeks had become thoroughly disillusioned with the war and only the recent bad weather had prevented them from leaving, but the day before the weather had changed and during the night a favourable wind had sprung up.

PRIAM was satisfied with the explanation but could not understand the presence of the wooden horse. SINON explained that when ODYSSEUS had stolen the Palladium from the temple of ATHENE, the Greeks had forfeited the support of the Goddess. With the wrath of ATHENE incurred, AGAMEMNON had decided to give up the battle and leave for home, leaving a gift for the Goddess, which they hoped would placate her.

PRIAM was still mystified as to why the horse was so big. SINON then told him that the Greeks had not wanted it taken inside the city walls, because it had been prophesied that, should the horse ever enter Troy, the Trojans would, with support from all over Asia, enjoy a victorious assault on Greece and the Mycenean Empire.

However, LAOCOON was still insistent that these were more lies and he wanted to burn the horse and sacrifice a bull to POSEIDON. At this point, APOLLO decided to intervene by sending two sea serpents to Troy which streaked ashore, coiled themselves around the twin sons of LAOCOON and crushed them to death. LAOCOON himself was killed in the same way, when he attempted to save the boys. PRIAM, satisfied with this action, decided that SINON had spoken the truth and immediately dedicated the gift to ATHENE. The horse was bedecked with flowers and a carpet of roses surrounded the hooves.

A great feast followed the apparent victory over the Greeks, which went on late into the night, until all were heavy with sleep. It was then that SINON crept from the city and lit a beacon on the tomb of ACHILLES. This was the signal that AGAMEMNON had been waiting for and the Greek fleet headed back to Troy.

Inside the city, the trap door in the horse opened and the Greeks came down the rope ladder, although the trembling EPEIUS needed coaxing. They overcame the sleepy guards before opening the city gates for AGAMEMNON's landing party. ODYSSEUS and his men systematically butchered the Trojans in their sleep and it fell to NEOPTOLEMUS, son of ACHILLES, to kill PRIAM on the steps of his palace, before dragging the body to

The Wooden Horse of Ttoy

his father's tomb, on which he draped the headless corpse. ODYSSEUS and MENELAUS, the husband of HELEN, rushed to the house of DEIPHOBUS, the son of PRIAM, where HELEN was staying and it was MENELAUS who killed DEIPHOBUS, reclaimed his wife and took her back to the ship.

The Trojans were all massacred, apart from just two families, those of ANTENOR and AENEAS, who had recently been urging PRIAM to give HELEN up to the Greeks and end the bloody siege.
PARIS, who had been the cause of the ten year struggle, through his elopement with HELEN, fell to the accurate aim of PHILOCTETES, who, you may recall, had inherited the famous bow and poisonous arrows of HERACLES. The three oracles which had been announced by ODYSSEUS had been fulfilled.

LITTLE AJAX insulted ATHENE when he attempted to abduct CASSANDRA, daughter of PRIAM, from the temple of the Goddess, dragging her away, still clutching ATHENE's image. As CASSANDRA was already claimed as the concubine of AGAMEMNON, ODYSSEUS proposed stoning LITTLE AJAX to death, but the would be abductor made a special plea for forgiveness to ATHENE and was temporarily spared. However, he was destined to die from a thunderbolt, which was given to the Goddess by her father, ZEUS.
Troy was burned to the ground and one of the last acts by the conquerors was the killing, by ODYSSEUS, of ASTYANAX, the infant son of HECTOR and the last surviving male of the House of Troy. It had been prophesied that, should the boy live, he would one day avenge the sacking of Troy and the death of his family. ODYSSEUS threw young ASTYANAX to his death from the battlement walls of the city.

HECABE, PRIAM's wife, sometimes known as HECUBA, was claimed by ODYSSEUS as his concubine, but she constantly cursed him for the crimes against both her family and her city. When he could stand it no longer, ODYSSEUS killed the bitter queen.

Besides CASSANDRA, the other surviving daughter of PRIAM was POLYXENA, who had once been admired and sought by ACHILLES, when he was alive. Now the ghost of ACHILLES appeared to his son, NEOPTOLEMUS, demanding that POLYXENA be sacrificed on his tomb, or else he would keep the Greek fleet becalmed at Troy, until his demand was satisfied. ODYSSEUS, with NEOPTOLEMUS acting as priest, duly sacrificed the princess and immediately after, winds sprang up to herald the departure of the fleet.

During the previous ten years, the Greeks had incurred the wrath of several Gods and Goddesses, in particular POSEIDON, and more recently, ATHENE. Between them, these two were to cause suffering and hardship to the returning Greeks. Many vessels were destroyed in violent storms and few Greek leaders had an easy passage, particularly ODYSSEUS, who knew from the Oracle that he was destined to roam the seas for the next decade, on his homeward journey.

The twelve ships under the command of ODYSSEUS were soon in trouble when, off the southern coast of the Peloponnese, they were caught by a fierce north wind and were blown off course for nine days. This took them to Libya, in North Africa. Here, on shore, ODYSSEUS sent out three scouts and, when they failed to return, he eventually discovered them in the village of a people known as the Lotus Eaters. This was a gentle, vegetarian tribe, whose chief diet was the lotus fruit, which had the effect of cancelling memory and instilling into the eater a desire for nothing more than to sit peacefully, nibbling the fruit all day long. Recognising the danger, ODYSSEUS dragged the three men back to the ship and at once set sail.

Many days later, they came to the island of the CYCLOPES, which is thought to be modern day Sicily. The CYCLOPES were giants with just a single eye in the middle of their foreheads.

Taking shelter on a smaller, off shore island, ODYSSEUS took his own ship, a dozen men and a few provisions, to investigate. With his twelve men, he climbed up to a large cave which he found to be unoccupied, but contained much food, besides a number of sheep and goats. They should have taken some supplies and left, but ODYSSEUS was curious to know who inhabited such a place. They soon found out when a one eyed giant appeared, entered the cave and sealed the entrance by rolling a huge boulder into the opening.

ODYSSEUS and his men hid in terror of this monster and were even more frightened when they were discovered. ODYSSEUS introduced themselves to the giant, POLYPHEMUS, as shipwrecked sailors, telling him that they should receive a hospitable welcome, as ordained by the Gods. POLYPHEMUS answered by saying that the CYCLOPES did not obey either the Gods or their laws and, as if to prove the point, he promptly swallowed two of the Greeks before going to sleep.

There was no escape from the cave and, after a fearsome night for ODYSSEUS and his companions, the giant awoke and gobbled another two men for his breakfast. Then, removing the boulder, he went out, taking his sheep and goats with him, before rolling the great stone back into place and imprisoning the men once more.

ODYSSEUS worked frantically on a plan of escape, which involved some excellent sweet wine which they had brought with their provisions. When POLYPHEMUS returned in the evening, he quickly ate two more Greeks for his supper before ODYSSEUS could offer him the wine. The giant enjoyed the wine and soon began to feel its pleasant effects. To obtain more wine, he promised ODYSSEUS (who he called OUDEIS, meaning nobody), a gift. On receipt of the nectar, the giant told ODYSSEUS that his gift was that he would be the last to be eaten, whereupon the wine had its desired effect and POLYPHEMUS fell into a deep sleep. ODYSSEUS fashioned a stake from olive wood and heated the point in the hot ashes of the fire. Then he drove the stake deep into the single eye of the sleeping giant and, with a twisting movement, gouged it out. The giant roared with pain which turned to anguish when he discovered that he was blind and, springing up, he rolled the boulder away from the opening, putting his arm across the entrance such that he could snatch the remaining Greeks should they attempt to escape.

The last part of ODYSSEUS' plan was put into effect. He strapped each of the six remaining to the underside of a ram and herded all the sheep to the entrance. Finally he took the largest ram and suspended himself beneath it, clinging by his hands and toes. When the blind giant felt the wollen backs of the sheep, he allowed them to go outside. He even registered surprise when the largest ram was the last to leave because it was normally the leader. So not only had ODYSSEUS managed to escape, but he had also captured the entire flock of sheep which he drove aboard his vessel before leaving to rejoin the rest of his ships.

However, ODYSSEUS could not resist shouting out and taunting the blind POLYPHEMUS, who retaliated by hurling a huge rock in the direction of the ship, but it fell some way ahead. The resulting wave almost drove them to the beach. ODYSSEUS bellowed to the giant;

'Should anyone ask you who blinded you, answer that it was not OUDEIS, but ODYSSEUS of Ithaca.'

The enraged POLYPHEMUS hurled another rock, but it fell short and this time the resulting wave helped the ship on its way. The grief stricken giant turned to his father POSEIDON and asked that, if his enemy ODYSSEUS ever reached his home, he would arrive late, on his own in a foreign ship and would find many problems waiting for him. POSEIDON promised to arrange things.

Travelling north, ODYSSEUS and his ships reached the island of AEOLUS, the Warden of the Winds, where they remained for about a month. AEOLUS wanted to help, so on their departure, he gave ODYSSEUS a leather bag which contained the North, South and East winds, securely tying its neck with silver wire, saying: 'The West wind is free and will drive you to your home in Ithaca. Should you need to change course for any reason, open the bag and select the appropriate assistance.

All went well until, within sight of Ithaca, a tragic event occurred. ODYSSEUS had fallen asleep and his crew, thinking that perhaps the bag, which he kept by his side, contained wine, opened it. The winds rushed out and drove the ship all the way back to AEOLUS. ODYSSEUS apologised and asked for further assistance from the West wind, but this time, AEOLUS, sensing that the Gods did not favour an easy passage for ODYSSEUS, told him to use his oars and be gone from the island.

After seven days, the ships arrived at Telepylus, where a race called the Laestrygonians lived. All the vessels, except for that of ODYSSEUS, tied up at the harbour mouth. A scouting party of three was sent ashore, meeting a young woman drawing water from a spring. Her father was the king of the island, she told them, and escorted them to the palace. Events turned grisly when the king devoured one of the scouts and the remaining two ran for their lives and to warn ODYSSEUS, who quickly untied and rowed towards the open sea. Tragically it was too late for the other eleven ships and their men. They were bombarded and sunk by the race of cannibals, before being speared and eaten.

Reduced to one ship, the despairing ODYSSEUS sailed on until he reached an island called Aeaea, off the western coast of Italy, in the vicinity of Rome. Hardly daring to investigate, following the disastrous visits to the Cyclopes and the Laestrygonians, it was some time before ODYSSEUS ventured ashore where, from a hill top, he spotted a solitary house. Returning to the ship, he divided the crew in two and they drew lots to see which group would form a landing party. The men led by one EURYLOCHUS were chosen and they cautiously began to explore. A few hours later, a desperate EURYLOCHUS returned alone, to report the disappearance of his party. He said that they had arrived at the house which ODYSSEUS had seen, to find it surrounded by wolves and lions which, strangely, did not attack them. From the house they could hear a woman singing, so they called to her and were invited in. They all entered, except for the uneasy EURYLOCHUS, unaware that the woman was CIRCE, a sorceress, who practised magic and dispensed drugs which could turn men and women into beasts. Inside, and unknown to EURYLOCHUS, the witch gave the men wine, touched them with a wand and turned them into pigs, which she herded into a sty and fed with swill. Outside

EURYLOCHUS waited in vain for his companions until, sensing that the worst had happened, he ran back to the ship. Reproaching the man for his cowardice, ODYSSEUS went on his own to discover what had happened to the party, on his way meeting a handsome young man who was actually HERMES in disguise. The youth told him who CIRCE was, warning him of her magic and what had happened to his crew members. Before leaving, he gave ODYSSEUS a plant with black roots and in white flower. It would act as an antidote to any potion the sorceress might give him.

As expected, CIRCE greeted the Hero with a drink, but armed with the protective plant, ODYSSEUS did not turn into a hog when touched with her wand. Instead, he drew his sword and threatened to kill her if she did not swear not to harm him. The sorceress vowed this to the Gods and, in fact, became the mistress of ODYSSEUS.

CIRCE threw a magic potion into the pig sty and ODYSSEUS' companions emerged, healthier and more handsome than before. Furthermore, she settled his crew comfortably with her handmaiden nymphs. So, after their unpleasant experiences, they all remained happily on the island until, after a year of idleness, they became restless for home.

CIRCE had promised to help ODYSSEUS and his men to reach Ithaca when the time came, and she explained that they would have to get the advice from the ghost of TEIRESIAS, a Theban seer, which dwelt in Hades. That meant a visit to the underworld and CIRCE gave ODYSSEUS precise instructions on how to get there. After a few days sailing, they came to Oceanus, the river which encircled the world. They came to rest in the land of the

Cimmerians, where the sun never shone and where they located a spot, described by CIRCE, where three underground rivers met. Here they dug a hole, into which they poured offerings of wine, milk and honey sprinkled with barley. Then they sacrificed a ram and a ewe, provided by CIRCE, dedicating the offering to HADES and his underworld wife, PERSEPHONE.

From the hole emerged spirits of the dead and ODYSSEUS, with drawn sword, had to prevent any of the ghosts from drinking the blood of the sacrificed animals, until the spirit of TEIRESIAS had been satisfied. This meant that he even had to refuse the spirit of his dead mother, ANTICLEIA.

When the ghost of the seer had drunk his fill, he told ODYSSEUS what things he could expect to happen and what he needed to do, if he and his crew were ever to reach Ithaca. In particular, he said that they should all be careful, when they reached an island called Thrinacia, not to touch any of the herds of flocks that belonged to HYPERION the Titan. If they did, then only ODYSSEUS would return home, in a foreign ship, to find his wife besieged by suitors. The ghost of the seer went on to say that, after ODYSSEUS arrived home, he would need to carry an oar on his shoulder to an area inland where the people ate their meat without salt. There, the oar would be mistaken for a winnowing tool and he should make a sacrifice to POSEIDON. He would then live a contented life in Ithaca and, eventually, the sea would be the cause of his death.

ODYSSEUS next satisfied his dead mother's thirst. She had died in his long absence and she gave him news of home, failing to mention the suitors who plagued PENELOPE. Numerous other spirits appeared, including those of AGAMEMNON, ACHILLES and GREAT AJAX.

AGAMEMNON warned ODYSSEUS to land on Ithaca unnoticed. ACHILLES was overjoyed to hear the news of the bravery shown by his son, NEOPTOLEMUS at Troy, while GREAT AJAX still had not forgiven the Hero for receiving the armour of the dead ACHILLES.

ODYSSEUS returned with his crew to Aeaea, where he was greeted by CIRCE, who was proud of him for having undertaken the daunting visit to Hades. She said, 'One death is enough for most men, but you will have two!' She told him that the next leg of their journey would take them past the island of the Sirens. These were two or possibly three creatures with the faces of young girls and the bodies of birds. They sang in such a seductive

manner, that whoever heard them was irresistibly attracted to them. Their singing had lured many mariners to their death on the rocks, where the Sirens sat among the bleached bones of dead sailors. CIRCE instructed ODYSSEUS to plug the ears of his crew with bees wax, but if he himself wanted to hear the music, he must first be securely tied to the mast of his ship and tell his men not to release him under any circumstances.

So this was the state they assumed as they neared the island. The sound of the beautiful voices reached the ears of ODYSSEUS with promises of all manner of desirable things. He strained to free himself, cursing the crew for not releasing him and even threatening to kill them. However, the more he struggled, the tighter grew his bindings and the ship passed the hazard without incident. It is said that the Sirens committed suicide, out of frustration.

A little further on lay the next obstacle, in the shape of a narrow passage between two cliffs. Beneath one cliff lurked the monster CHARYBDIS, who, three times a day, sucked in a huge quantity of water before spitting it out, thereby creating a gigantic whirlpool. The other cliff housed SCYLLA, the once beautiful daughter of HECATE, who had been transformed into a monstrous dog, which had six heads and twelve feet. It lived in a cave in the side of the cliff and posed a threat to any passing ship.

ODYSSEUS decided that his best course was to steer clear of CHARYBDIS, for fear of being sucked into the whirlpool, which meant that he had to pass close to the cliff of SCYLLA. In fact the reckless ODYSSEUS went too close and six heads suddenly appeared over the side of the ship, which, when they withdrew, each carried a sailor in its jaw, snatched from his oars. The screams of these men were heartbreaking, but there was nothing ODYSSEUS could do but hurry on through the narrow passage.

The depleted crew rowed on, to reach Thrinacia, the land where HYPERION grazed his immortal cattle, which ODYSSEUS had been warned not to touch. Here they were land locked and unable to leave. Provisions grew scarce, hunting and fishing were unproductive and, in desperation, EURYLOCHUS incited some of the men to join him, to steal some of the cattle. Waiting until ODYSSEUS was asleep, they slaughtered several of the herd, roasting the meat and offering the thigh bones and fat to the Gods. Hoping to placate HYPERION, they promised to build a temple to the Titan, on their return to Ithaca.

When ODYSSEUS woke he was horrified to learn what had happened and feared the terrible wrath of HYPERION who had already complained to ZEUS of his loss. So he gathered his men and they left the island quickly. They had not gone very far, however, when they were made to feel the full might of ZEUS' anger. The God sent a storm which caused the collapse of the main mast, crushing the helmsman to death. ZEUS then hurled a thunder bolt at the ship, which capsized and sank with the loss of all hands, except for ODYSSEUS, who lashed the broken mast and keel together, making a floating structure to climb on. A southerly wind blew him back towards the dreaded CHARYBDIS and he was only saved by clinging to a wild fig tree, when his makeshift raft was sucked under. After a while, the raft was regurgitated and, retrieving it, he was able to carry on. For nine days he drifted aimlessly until he arrived at the island of Ogygia, where, in a great cavern, lived the beautiful Goddess, CALYPSO, together with her handmaidens. CALYPSO posed no threat to ODYSSEUS, other than her desire that he remain with her for ever, in return for which she would make him both ageless and immortal. ODYSSEUS spent seven years with CALYPSO, but he dreamed of home and his wife, PENELOPE, who he knew would be waiting for him. It needed the combined efforts of ZEUS, ATHENE and HERMES, to smooth the way for a return journey. The Gods had decided that the Hero had suffered enough, so ATHENE visited his son, TELEMACHUS, on Ithaca, to help contain the many household problems, while ZEUS sent the diplomatic God, HERMES, both to persuade CALYPSO to part with ODYSSEUS and to console her over his loss. CALYPSO produced tools that allowed ODYSSEUS to build a small boat, which was packed with provisions for the forthcoming journey. With many tears, she and the two sons of the union, NAUSINOUS and NAUSITHOUS, said their goodbyes.

ODYSSEUS sailed for seventeen days, before reaching sight of the island of Scherie. It was then that POSEIDON sent a violent storm which wrecked the boat and would have sent ODYSSEUS to a watery grave, had it not been for the timely appearance and intervention of the sea Goddess, LEUCOTHEA. She advised the Hero to remove his sodden clothes and put his faith in swimming. Before she left him, she gave him her veil which, stretched underneath him, gave added buoyancy. ATHENE sent a north wind to assist him and after two days he beached at the mouth of a river, on the island of Scherie where, as instructed, he returned the veil of LEUCOTHEA to the sea, before falling into a deep sleep.

ODYSSEUS' protectress, ATHENE, then arranged that he be discovered. She achieved this by ensuring that NAUSICAA, the daughter of the island's king, would enjoy a day out by the river with her handmaidens, where they combined the laundering of their clothes with a picnic. It was the noise of this party that woke ODYSSEUS and he requested their help. He was taken to the King who, having learned who he was and hearing of his plight, agreed to transport him to Ithaca with escorts who knew the route and the island well. Together with many gifts they left the next day, arriving at the harbour of Ithaca after a short journey. ODYSSEUS was in a deep sleep when they gently placed him on the beach, along with his presents. However, their kind deed turned to tragedy when, on their return journey and within sight of their island of Scherie, POSEIDON punished them for the help given to ODYSSEUS. He turned the ship and its occupants to stone.

ODYSSEUS, left on the beach, still needed the help of ATHENE. She came to him disguised as a shepherd boy and was highly amused at his false tales of how he came to be there. Laughing at his accomplished lies, she revealed herself to him. After stowing his gifts in a cave, ATHENE transformed his appearance, giving him grey hair, a wrinkled skin and clothing him in rags. She directed him to the shed of EUMAEUS, the palace swine herd.

Now ODYSSEUS was completely ignorant of the situation which had developed in Ithaca during his twenty year absence. On the general assumption that he would not return or even that he was dead, more than one hundred princes were seeking the hand of his faithful wife, PENELOPE, knowing that the lucky suitor would also gain the throne of Ithaca on the death of King LAERTES. Furthermore, these princes were planning to murder TELEMACHUS, the son of ODYSSEUS, who at that time was in Sparta, seeking news of his father from MENELAUS.

PENELOPE insisted to her suitors that an oracle had forecast her husband's eventual return. She promised, however, that she would select one of them as a partner, when she had completed the task of weaving a shroud for old LAERTES, which would guard him against death. To spin out the time, every evening she would unravel most of the day's work, so after three years, very little had been done. During this time, the suitors were living off the produce of the palace and seducing the maid servants.

ODYSSEUS, in conversation with the swineherd, EUMAEUS, who of course did not recognise him, told him that ODYSSEUS was alive and would soon be home, whereupon EUMAEUS went to the palace with the news. Meanwhile, ATHENE caused the return of TELEMACHUS, ensuring that he went straight to his father, when she reversed the disguise and there was a joyous reunion between father and son. ODYSSEUS asked his son to keep the secret from his mother for a while, and in his disguise once more, he set off for the palace to view the situation, achieving this by pretending to be a beggar, asking scraps from all the princes, who abused him and even threw a stool at him. PENELOPE was summoned to the disturbance and when EUMAEUS told her that the beggar had news of her husband, she arranged to see him in the royal parlour that same evening. Apart from TELEMACHUS, no one knew him at this stage, except for his old dog, who wagged his tail in recognition of his master. Then, as if the hound had been waiting for that moment, it closed its eyes and contentedly died of old age.

When the suitors had retired for the evening, ODYSSEUS and his son took all the weapons from the walls of the banqueting hall and stored them in the cellars. Then ODYSSEUS went, as promised, to the royal parlour, for his meeting with PENELOPE. There he told her that her husband had gone to Dodona to consult the oracle of ZEUS and would soon be home. PENELOPE announced that she could delay no further and intended to hold a contest to select a partner. The competitors would have to let fly an arrow so accurately that it would pass through the rings of

twelve axes set in a straight row, a feat that her husband
ODYSSEUS used to perform. The bow to be used by all
belonged to her husband, presented to him twenty five
years previously by IPHITUS, the unfortunate young man
who had been killed by HERACLES, the crime costing that
great Hero the penalty of three years in bondage.
ODYSSEUS told PENELOPE that the contest was a good
idea and he was sure that her husband would be back in
time to compete.

PENELOPE then ordered that the beggar's feet be washed
by the aged nurse, EURYCLEIA, who had looked after
ODYSSEUS as a boy. While performing this task, the old
woman noticed a scar on his thigh, caused in his youth by a
wild boar, ODYSSEUS was only just in time to stop her
from announcing his safe return and asked her to keep it a
secret for a while.

A feast was held the following day and, after the banquet,
PENELOPE brought out the bow and had the twelve axes
placed in position, announcing that the winner of the
competion would receive her hand in marriage.

TELEMACHUS attempted to string the bow and when he
failed, the suitors tried in turn, but all were unsuccessful.
While this was in progress, ODYSSEUS found the palace
servants and told them who he was, thus preparing them,
because they all had a part to play in the events to come,
which he had planned carefully with his son. Then, still in
the guise of a beggar, he asked that he might have a turn at
stringing the bow. He was subject to much ridicule but
PENELOPE insisted that he be given the opportunity. At
this point, TELEMACHUS asked his mother if he might
speak to her in private and they left the hall, when
ATHENE put PENELOPE into a deep sleep. Back in the
hall, ODYSSEUS strung the bow with comparative ease and

shot an arrow which passed cleanly through the twelve axe holes.

Positioning himself in the doorway and joined by his son, ODYSSEUS let fly the arrows at the princes, who in their turn rushed for the spears normally hanging on the walls, only to find them gone. One by one they fell from the deadly aim and the slaughter continued until all but three lay dead. Of these, two were spared for kindnesses they alone had shown to the old beggar, while the third, who had attempted to arm the suitors, was severely mutilated, his extremities being cut off and fed to the hounds. ODYSSEUS fumigated the palace with sulphur, washed the blood from his person and revealed himself to all by removing his disguise.

ODYSSEUS was at last reunited with his faithful wife and his overjoyed father, LAERTES, but the happy situation was short lived. A legal action was brought against the Hero by the combined families of the dead princes, the appointed judge being the son of ACHILLES, NEOPTOLEMUS. The ruling was that ODYSSEUS had to leave his kingdom and not return for ten years. While he was away, the heirs of the dead suitors had to pay compensation for their years of plunder, to TELEMACHUS, who would reign as king in his father's absence. So the prophecy of the Theban seer, given to ODYSSEUS on his mission to the underworld, became fact and ODYSSEUS set out across the Pindos mountains, carrying an oar across his shoulder.

While ODYSSEUS was away, an oracle predicted to PENELOPE that he would be killed by his own son, so she had TELEMACHUS exiled and took the throne herself. The lonely, unfortunate ODYSSEUS, early in his wanderings, met a crowd in a village square, where someone called to him,

'Stranger, why a winnowing bat in springtime?'

This strange cry reminded him of a part of TEIRESIAS' prophecy, so he promptly made a sacrifice, on the spot, to POSEIDON, of a bull, a boar and a ram. So ended the terrible wrath of the God who was appeased and gave ODYSSEUS his forgiveness.

It was a further nine years before the Hero could return and it is said that, during this time, he married the queen of the Thresprotians, CALLIDICE, commanding her forces in battle against the region known as Brygia, in Epirus, whose own army was led by the God of War himself, ARES. The battle resulted in honour on both sides, as APOLLO called a truce.

ODYSSEUS eventually returned to Ithaca and his wife, PENELOPE, where the final, tragic scene unfolded. During the time that CIRCE and ODYSSEUS had lived together, they had produced a son, TELEGONUS, who was now on a mission to find his father, but was also raiding islands on his travels, in order to secure provisions. TELEGONUS, thinking that he had reached Corcyra, had in fact arrived at Ithaca, and ODYSSEUS led a force to repel the pirates. On the beach, ODYSSEUS was speared to death, the spear armed with the spine of a sting ray, the assailant being his own son, TELEGONUS. Both the oracle and the prophecy had been fulfilled.

In conclusion, TELEGONUS spent a year in exile for the killing, after which it was he who married PENELOPE and reigned over Ithaca. As for TELEMACHUS, he married none other than CIRCE; thus a close knot was drawn, tying together the continuing threads of the family of ODYSSEUS, a remarkable, long suffering and memorable Hero.

Part 8

ORPHEUS

PROMETHEUS
TITAN Son of IAPETUS

PANDORA
First mortal woman (AllGifts)

PYRRHA
Daughter of PANDORA and EPIMETHEUS

DEUCALION
Ruler of PHTHIA

HELLEN
Ancestor of the HellenicRace

ORSEIS
Nymph

AEOLUS
Ancestor of the Aeolian Race

ENARETE
Virtuous

MAGNES
Ancestor of the MAGNESIANS PELION area of THESSALY

METHONE
Nymph

PIERUS
King of PELLA

OEAGRUS
King of THRACE

CALLIOPE
The MUSE OF EPIC POETRY

ORPHEUS

ORPHEUS was the greatest poet and musician who ever lived. His mother was CALLIOPE, reputedly the senior of the nine Muses and specifically the Muse of Epic Poetry. His father was the Thracian king, OEAGRUS, which explains why he was always referred to as the Thracian Poet.

His musical instrument was the lyre, given to him by APOLLO, the Muses teaching him to play the instrument. Such was the quality of his music that wild beasts became calm when they heard it, while trees and even rocks danced and followed him.

You may recall that he joined JASON on his famous quest for the Golden Fleece and it was the calming effect of his music which maintained the harmony of the crew for most of the voyage.

ORPHEUS married the Naiad nymph, EURYDICE, who met a tragic death when a shepherd named ARISTAEUS, a lustful young man who tended the flocks of the Muses, chased her. Poor EURYDICE, in her haste to get away, trod on a snake and died of the poisonous bite.

ORPHEUS was grief stricken and determined to get her back. He descended into the underworld where he successfully negotiated the ferryman, CHARON, the guardian dog CERBERUS with the three heads and even the three ruling judges, MINOS, RHADAMANTHYS and AEACUS. They were all charmed, almost hypnotised by his music and HADES himself was so overcome by his playing that he gave ORPHEUS permission to take EURYDICE back with him to the upper world. The only condition he imposed was that, on the return journey, he was not to look back, under any circumstances, until they reached the light of day.

Comforted by the playing of his lyre,
EURYDICE followed ORPHEUS through
the long, dark passage. When they had
almost reached the exit, ORPHEUS, in his
excitement, turned to make sure that his
wife was following him. In a moment of
forgetfulness, he had ignored the condition
set by HADES and poor EURYDICE faded
back into the underworld for ever.

It is said that, in remaining faithful to the
memory of his beloved EURYDICE,
ORPEHUS never again sought the love of a
woman, some going so far as to say that he
openly preached homosexual love.

However, on his return to Thrace.
ORPHEUS became a priest in APOLLO's
temple and he worshipped the sun God,
HELIOS, whom he greeted each morning
at dawn from the summit of Mount
Pangaeum. His views and beliefs were
completely opposed to those of DIONYSUS

and when that God came to Thrace, he was angered that ORPHEUS did not honour him or show some respect.

Now the female votaries of DIONYSUS were known as Maenads or Bacchantes who, in an orgiastic frenzy, would incite the same state into the local women wherever the God's travels took him. They all became wild, lost control of their senses and, dressed in skins, were a fearful sight. The husbands of the Thracian women, distressed by the wild drunkeness of their womenfolk, went to the temple of APOLLO to attend a service given by ORPHEUS, when DIONYSUS armed and then incited the demented wives into action. They burst into the building and slaughtered their menfolk. As for poor ORPHEUS, they tore him limb from limb and threw his head into a nearby river.

ORPHEUS' limbs were retrieved by the sorrowful Muses, who buried them at the foot of Mount Olympus, in a place where, it is said, the nightingales sing sweeter than any other place in the world. As for his head, it sang all the way down river to the sea, finally coming to rest on the island of Lesbos, where the islanders kindly buried it. His lyre was immortalised in the sky as the constellation Lyra and the Gods punished the devilish Maenads by turning them into a grove of oak trees. ORPHEUS continued to be worshipped and, much later, about the sixth century BC his cult, called Orphism, strangely influenced the philosophy of PYTHAGORAS.

Part 9

AGAMEMNON AND ORESTES

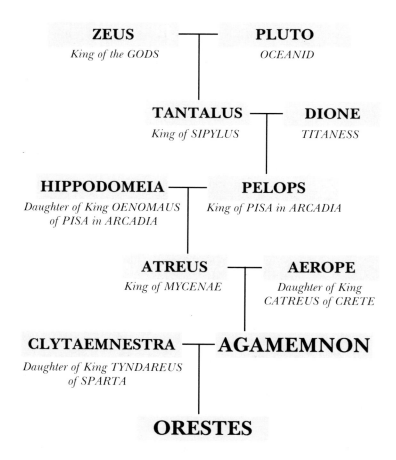

ZEUS
King of the GODS

PLUTO
OCEANID

TANTALUS
King of SIPYLUS

DIONE
TITANESS

HIPPODOMEIA
Daughter of King OENOMAUS of PISA in ARCADIA

PELOPS
King of PISA in ARCADIA

ATREUS
King of MYCENAE

AEROPE
Daughter of King CATREUS of CRETE

CLYTAEMNESTRA
Daughter of King TYNDAREUS of SPARTA

AGAMEMNON

ORESTES

ATREUS, to whom ZEUS had endowed untold wealth, was king of Mycenae, founder of the House of Atreus and the father of AGAMEMNON. ATREUS ruled the whole of the Mycenaean Empire, where he and his brother, THYESTES, had vied for the throne for many years. Eventually, AEGISTHUS, the son of THYESTES, murdered ATREUS to help his father become king, but King TYNDARAEUS of Sparta, a close ally of ATREUS, deposed THYESTES, returning the kingdom to AGAMEMNON, who took his place as rightful heir, the King of Mycenae and the most powerful ruler in the land.

AGAMEMNON married CLYTAEMNESTRA, the daughter of King TYNDAREUS and they had four children, a son, ORESTES and three daughters, ELECTRA, IPHIGENIA and CHRYSOTHEMIS. To complete the family, AGAMEMNON's brother, MENELAUS, married CLYTAEMNESTRA'S sister, HELEN.

Now when HELEN eloped with PARIS to Troy, it was to AGAMEMNON that her husband, MENELAUS, turned for help, to effect her recapture, thus restoring honour to Greece.

All the princes who had courted the beautiful HELEN, before her marriage to MENELAUS, were marshalled, as they had sworn loyalty to whichever partner she finally selected. These helped to form an army and navy which sailed to Troy under the respective leadership of AGAMEMNON and ACHILLES. The overall leader of the expedition was AGAMEMNON, a task which was to occupy him for ten years.

The expedition had a false start, but when the Greek fleet .was assembled for the second time at Aulis, ready to sail for

Troy, AGAMEMNON is said to have insulted the Goddess of Hunting, ARTEMIS, when boasting that his skills as a hunter were superior to hers. As a punishment, the fleet was becalmed at Aulis and it was prophesied that, in order to obtain a favourable wind, AGAMEMNON would have to sacrifice his daughter, IPHIGENIA, to the Goddess.

AGAMEMNON, under extreme pressure from his generals and with his leadership threatened, reluctantly had to agree. IPHIGENIA was brought to Aulis on the pretext that she was to marry ACHILLES, who refused to be party to the plot, swearing to defend the young girl, although it is said that she was nevertheless prepared to die for the honour of Greece. It was at the last minute, when IPHIGENIA was lying on the sacrificial altar, that ARTEMIS relented and took the girl to Tauris, where she became the chief priestess to the Goddess. The promised wind sprung up and the fleet set sail for Troy.

The Trojan expedition sailed without AGAMEMNON's cousin and sworn enemy, AEGISTHUS, who not only did not join the force, but, in the absence of AGAMEMNON, also became the lover of CLYTAEMNESTRA. She was not difficult to seduce as she disliked AGAMEMNON intensely, having originally been claimed by him from her first husband, TANTALUS, whom he killed, along with their baby, snatched from the breast and dashed to death.

The two lovers plotted to murder AGAMEMNON on his return. CLYTAEMNESTRA's hatred of her husband increased with the knowledge that he had been prepared to sacrifice their daughter, IPHIGENIA, and with the news from Troy that he had taken King PRIAM's daughter, CASSANDRA, as his concubine.

A message was sent to AGAMEMNON, telling him to light a beacon on his way home, if he was victorious. This would set off a train of beacons, and a guard was posted day and night on the palace roof, with his eye fixed on Mount Arachneon, which towered between the city and the Saronic Gulf. Thus CLYTAEMNESTRA was warned of her husband's homecoming

Despite the fact that he was accompanied by CASSANDRA, when AGAMEMNON eventually arrived home, his wife greeted him with delight and informed him that a warm bath was prepared, to ease his weary body after the arduous journey. CASSANDRA, a prophetess, remained outside, having a premonition of the tragedy that was about to unfold.

After he had bathed, CLYTAEMNESTRA rushed towards her husband with a towel, as if to dry him, but instead threw a net over him. Before he could disentangle himself, AEGISTHUS came out of hiding and killed him with mighty blows of his sword. AGAMEMNON fell back into the bath, whereupon CLYTAEMNESTRA cut off his head. She rushed to find CASSANDRA whose head also rolled.

During the melee that followed between AEGISTHUS' warriors, who attacked the citadel, and the loyal guards of AGAMEMNON, ELECTRA, together with her father's old tutor, made her escape, taking with her ORESTES, her ten year old brother.

Full of grief for her dead father, ELECTRA married a poor and aged peasant. The marriage was not consummated and she lived a life of abject poverty, refusing to forgive her mother and AEGISTHUS for their brutal crime.

AEGISTHUS reigned for the next seven years at Mycenae, but lived in fear of a prophecy which had stated that ORESTES would one day avenge his father's murder.

ORESTES himself was taken, by the old tutor, to the court of STROPHIUS, who had married AGAMEMNON's sister. There he grew up in the company of his cousin, PYLADES and they became inseparable companions.

ELECTRA urged ORESTES, with constant messages, to avenge the death of their father. So, when he reached manhood, ORESTES consulted the Delphic Oracle on the matter. The Oracle's answer, in the name of APOLLO and blessed by ZEUS, was that, if he failed to avenge his father's death, he would become a leper and an outcast. There was no doubt in the minds of the Gods as to what needed to be done. They instructed ORESTES to go to AGAMEMNON's tomb and place upon it a lock of his hair. Then, unaided, he was to kill the two murderers. He was warned that in doing so, he would be guilty of matricide and could therefore expect to be tormented by the ERINNYES, or FURIES, the female spirits who punished anyone who committed a crime against their own blood kin. Finally, the oracle told ORESTES that, should the ERINNYES make life unbearable for him, he was to return to Delphi and seek the help of APOLLO.

Accompanied by PYLADES, ORESTES journeyed to Mycenae and placed a ringlet of his hair on his father's tomb, hiding behind a nearby bush when a party of peasant women arrived. The group of women, which included ELECTRA, poured libations on the tomb when ELECTRA, noticing the ringlet of hair, realised that ORESTES had arrived. He made himself known to her and there was a tearful yet joyous reunion.

Meanwhile, CLYTAEMNESTRA had had a nightmare, in which she gave birth to a serpent that drew blood from her breast. She consulted a seer and was told that she had incurred the wrath of the dead, a story that soon became general knowledge and ORESTES, hearing the tale, likened himself to the serpent.

ELECTRA was asked by ORESTES to visit her mother, but to say nothing of his coming. After a short time, he arrived at the palace unaccompanied, and begged food and shelter, posing as a Phocian and adopting the accent of those people. Knowing that AEGISTHUS could not refuse the customary hospitality, he asked at the gate for the master or mistress and was received by his mother, who failed to recognise him. He told her that he had brought a message from AGAMEMNON's brother-in-law, STROPHIUS, which said that her son, ORESTES, was dead and STROPHIUS wanted to know what he should do with the ashes, which were contained in a bronze urn. Secretly overjoyed, CLYTAEMNESTRA sent the old nurse, GEILISSA, to fetch AEGISTHUS. The nurse, who had recognised ORESTES, told AEGISTHUS, when she found him, that he could rejoice in the news that his enemy was dead, so he had nothing to worry about any more. She asked him to kindly join CLYTAEMNESTRA, telling him that there was no need to arm himself. Just as AEGISTHUS entered the hall, there was a knock and PYLADES was admitted, carrying a bronze urn, saying that it contained the ashes of ORESTES and that he was delivering it on behalf of STROPHIUS.

The distraction was all that ORESTES needed. He cut down AEGISTHUS with his sword, then, with a fearsome stroke, he removed his mother's head. Standing over the bodies, he announced to the palace staff that he had avenged the death of his father by taking the lives of the murderous adulterers, and asked for their loyalty and support. Almost immediately, the ERINNYES appeared and began to torment and attack ORESTES like a plague of horse flies. The dog-headed and bat-winged ERINNYES were relentless and he spent the next week lying down, covered up, with neither sleep nor food.

King TYNDAREUS arrived from Sparta and charged ORESTES with matricide and ELECTRA with complicity. Left to him, he would have had both of them stoned to death, but a trial took place,

The sword of Orestes

with PYLADES also accused of conspiring to murder. Influencing the court was MENELAUS, who arrived accompanied by his wife, HELEN and their daughter, HERMIONE. In a cowardly manner he refused to support ORESTES' actions. The verdict was guilty and all three were sentenced to commit suicide, but they decided that, if they were going to die, they would make sure that the Spartan dynasty would also suffer.

ORESTES attempted to murder HELEN in revenge for the attitude of MENELAUS, but the Gods intervened and spirited her away to Olympus, where she became the immortal guardian of sailors in distress. Next, ORESTES and ELECTRA attempted to kill HERMIONE, but APOLLO appeared to save her and the God decided to handle the situation himself from then on. He duly decreed that MENELAUS should take another wife and that HERMIONE should be betrothed to ORESTES. Furthermore, he informed MENELAUS that the murder of CLYTAEMNESTRA need no longer concern him, as the Gods would deal with the matter.

ORESTES, plagued by the ERINNYES, made his way to Delphi, to seek help from APOLLO, who advised him to face his suffering with courage and, following a one year period of exile, to make his way to Athens and embrace the image of ATHENE. It was only ATHENE, with her dreaded aegis, embellished with the head of the gorgon MEDUSA, who could dispel the ERINNYES.

During his year of exile, the period decreed in those days to atone for a killing, the wretched ORESTES was almost driven insane by the ceaseless bombardment of the ERINNYES. He trudged from place to place, constantly seeking purification, which, when received, only gave temporary comfort. APOLLO, HERMES and even ZEUS occasionally eased his suffering and monuments, still in evidence today, mark the various places in the Peloponnese where ORESTES enjoyed some relief from his torment. At last the year was up and he journeyed to Athens, going straight to the Temple of ATHENE and embracing her image.

Then an extraordinary trial took place, presided over by ATHENE, the prosecution being represented by the elder ERINNYE and the defence by APOLLO. APOLLO presented his case, defending the matricide by lessening the importance of motherhood. He said that the father was the supreme authority, the woman only providing a reception area and incubation period for his seed. The verdict of not guilty was eventually decided by the casting vote of the virgin goddess, who sided with APOLLO. So ORESTES was

aquitted and in thanks to ATHENE, he dedicated an altar to her honour.

Now many of the ERINNYES were unable to accept the verdict and continued to pester ORESTES. So in despair he returned once more to Delphi, threatening suicide if APOLLO did not help him. The Oracle told him to sail to the Black Sea, where at Tauris he would find the temple to ARTEMIS. From there he had to steal a wooden image of the Goddess and take it to Attica.

The Taurians were a savage people. One of their customs was the sacrifice of any sailor who had either been shipwrecked off their coast or driven into their harbour by a storm. The temple was an awesome sight and its white marble altar was always stained with blood.

Together with PYLADES, ORESTES set out to comply with the oracle's instructions, commissioning a ship of fifty oars for the journey. Anchoring off the Taurian coast, the two men slipped ashore and hid in a cave, preparing to raid the temple after night fall. They were discovered by herdsmen, who thought that they were some immortal beings, or even the DIOSCURI, twin half brothers of who you will hear more. All would have been well, but ORESTES was afflicted by a mad spell, when he began howling like a mad dog and the herdsmen realised that they were just ordinary mortals. The two were taken as prisoners to the Temple of ARTEMIS, for immediate sacrifice, as was the custom.

You will recall that ORESTES' sister, IPHEGENIA, who was to have been sacrificed to ARTEMIS at Aulis, had been saved by the Goddess and installed as her chief priestess in Tauris, a position whose duties included the sole charge of the sacred wooden image of ARTEMIS. ORESTES had no idea that his sister was still alive, believing that the sacrifice had been carried out to lift the curse from the Greek fleet.

The sacrificial ceremony was conducted by IPHIGENIA, who soon realised that it was her brother lying before her. To save him and his companion, PYLADES, she devised a plan. She announced that, as ORESTES had committed matricide, he was not fit material for sacrifice. She would have to take the two prisoners, together with the wooden image of ARTEMIS, to the sea, for cleansing. While she was doing this, she said, the king of Taurus had to arrange the purification of the temple, ordering the citizens to remain indoors, thus preventing their contamination by the prisoners. After this, said IPHIGENIA, all would be ready for the sacrifice.

So ORESTES, PLYADES and IPHIGENIA, with the wooden image of ARTEMIS, went down to the beach and boarded the ship. As they were leaving, there was a brief struggle to repel certain Taurian guards who suspected that they were being tricked. Another disaster might also have ruined their escape, in the shape of a storm, if POSEIDON had not intervened to calm the seas at the special request of ATHENE. The ship reached the island of Zminthe, where ATHENE appeared to ORESTES with final instructions. He was to place the wooden statue in a temple to ARTEMIS TAUROPOLUS, which had to be built in honour of the Goddess at Brauron in Attica.

IPHIGENIA was to became the chief Priestess of the new temple. While it was being built, she accompanied her

brother to Delphi, to be reunited with their sister,
ELECTRA.
ELECTRA returned with IPHIGENIA to Athens, where
she married PYLADES.

As for ORESTES, there are many stories told about what
happened to him, but the version we have chosen is that he
joined HERMIONE in Sparta, where they were married
and he became king of that powerful region, on the death
of MENELAUS. In addition, while he had been in exile, it
was rumoured at Mycenae that he had died. So the
Mycenaean throne had been claimed by ALETES, the son
of AEGISTHUS and CLYTAEMNESTRA.

ORESTES finally avenged the murders of his father and
grandfather when he killed ALETES and reclaimed the
throne for the House of Atreus. He became a powerful
leader and added many regions of the Peloponnese to his
already substantial empires of Sparta and Mycenae. He was
seventy years old when a Delphic oracle commanded him to
leave his kingdoms and go to live in Arcadia. It was there
that he died of a snake bite and, in conclusion, it is not
difficult to associate this event with the dream that his
mother had, just before he killed her.

Part 10

OEDIPUS

ZEUS — **IO**

King of the Gods *Daughter of INACHUS
the Argive RiverGod*

EPHASUS — **MEMPHIS**

Founder of Memphis *Daughter of the
GOD NILE*

POSEIDON — **LIBYA**

God of the Sea *The Goddess of Libya*

AGENOR — **TELEPHASSA**

*King of Sidon
in Phoenicia* *A moon Goddess*

HARMONIA — **CADMUS**

*Daughter of ARES
and APHRODITE* *King of Thebes*

POLYDORUS — **NYCTEIS**

King of Thebes *Daughter of NYCTEUS*

LABDACUS

King of Thebes.

JOCASTA — **LAIUS**

*Daughter of MENOECEUS
King of Thebes a Theban Noble* *King of Thebes*

OEDIPUS

OEDIPUS was the only son of King LAIUS of Thebes and JOCASTA, the daughter of a Theban nobleman. As LAIUS was warned by an oracle that one day he would be killed by his own son, he took the baby to Mount Cithaeron, where he pierced its feet, tied them together and left the child to die. Luckily, however, the infant was found by a shepherd, who took it to POLYBUS, the king of Corinth, who adopted it, naming the boy OEDIPUS, which means 'swollen foot'.

When OEDIPUS was a young man he was taunted by a drinking companion for not being a true son of King POLYBUS. This troubled him, so he went to consult the Delphic oracle, where he was told that one day he would kill his father and marry his mother. OEDIPUS loved POLYBUS and his wife MEROPE, believing them to be his parents and he decided that, if he left home, he might cheat the prediction, thus preventing the unthinkable from happening. So, reluctantly, he left Corinth and headed towards Delphi, knowing that he would never return again.

It was at a road junction near Delphi, that the driver of a chariot, coming from the opposite direction, ordered OEDIPUS off the path. OEDIPUS ignored the high handed order and the chariot and its entourage came on, the driver hitting the young man with his crop and the wheel of the carriage grazing his foot. In a rage, OEDIPUS killed both the driver and his servant and, leaving the bodies to be cleared by the rest of the party, he continued on his way.

Eventually OEDIPUS arrived at Thebes, at a time when its people were being terrorised by a female monster known as the SPHINX, which had the body of a lion, the wings of a bird and the face and bust of a woman. This monster would ask its intended victims to answer a riddle and, when they failed to give the correct reply, would devour them. No one was safe. Even the queen had lost a nephew. An oracle had stated that Thebes would not be rid of the SPHINX until the riddle had been solved. The situation in the city deteriorated when a member of the royal party arrived to report the death of the king, LAIUS, who had been attacked and killed while on the way to Delphi to consult the Pythian oracle.

The Sphinx

That meant that CREON, the king's brother in law, who had been put in charge of Thebes by LAIUS before he left, assumed the throne.

In absolute terror of the monster, CREON decreed that both the throne and the hand of the widowed queen, JOCASTA, would go to the man who could solve the riddle and relieve Thebes of the SPHINX.

OEDIPUS, a bright young man, decided to pit his wits against a certain death. The riddle, when put to him, ran thus:
'Which animal has four feet in the morning, two at midday and three in the evening?'
OEDIPUS answered,
'Man, who in infancy crawls on all fours, in maturity walks upright on two legs and who requires the assistance of a walking stick in old age.'

The defeated SPHINX threw itself from the city walls to its death and OEDIPUS claimed his prize, becoming the husband of JOCASTA and King of Thebes. The oracle had been fulfilled. OEDIPUS had unknowingly killed his true father and married his own mother.

By JOCASTA, OEDIPUS had four children, two sons, ETEOCLES and POLYNEICES and two daughters, ANTIGONE and ISMENE. He had reigned successfully for twenty years when a terrible plague fell on the city, accompanied by a severe drought. Hundreds were dying and CREON was sent to Delphi to consult the oracle. He was told that the man who killed LAIUS still lived, unpunished, in Thebes and, until he was detected and banished from the region, the plague would not end.

When OEDIPUS heard the news, he immediately pronounced a curse on the murderer of LAIUS, sentenced him to be exiled and set himself the task of discovering the identity of the offender. The terrible chain of events was uncovered when the investigation attracted the attention of the member of LAIUS' party who, on the day of the attack, had brought the news of the King's death to Thebes. TEIRESIAS, the wisest seer in the land, was called and the shepherd who had originally found the abandoned child of LAIUS, came to testify. Poor, tragic OEDIPUS learned that he had killed his father and was married to his own mother.

JOCASTA, on hearing the truth, in her shame and distress, hung herself. The distraught OEDIPUS, taking a brooch from her gown, gouged out his own eyes. Left to live with the horror of the situation, he went into exile, dressed in rags and accompanied by his faithful daughter ANTIGONE, who led her blind father by the hand.

Eventually the pair reached Colonus, a suburb of Athens, where, after many years of mental torment, OEDIPUS was finally purified of his crimes. As if by a command from the Gods, he simply vanished one day, perhaps a sign that he was eventually rewarded with immortality.

Part 11
MINOS

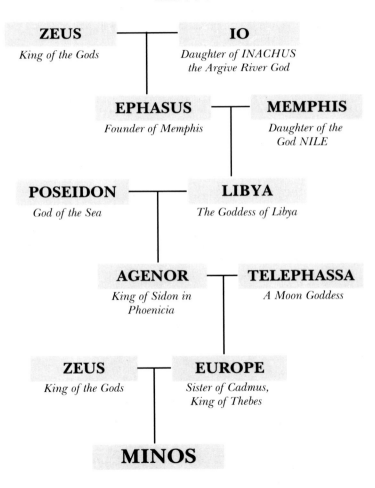

ZEUS

King of the Gods

IO

Daughter of INACHUS the Argive River God

EPHASUS

Founder of Memphis

MEMPHIS

Daughter of the God NILE

POSEIDON

God of the Sea

LIBYA

The Goddess of Libya

AGENOR

King of Sidon in Phoenicia

TELEPHASSA

A Moon Goddess

ZEUS

King of the Gods

EUROPE

Sister of Cadmus, King of Thebes

MINOS

DAEDALUS AND ICARUS

HEPHAESTUS ———— **ATTHIS**

The SMITH God

Daughter of King CRANAUS of Athens. From her name derives the region of ATTICA.

ERICHTHONIOS ——— **PRAXITHEA "A"**

King of Athens

NAIAD NYMPH

ZEUXIPPE ——— **PANDION 1**

NAIAD NYMPH. Sister of PRAXITHEA 'A"

King of Athens

ERECHTHEUS ——— **PRAXITHEA "B"**

King of Athens

Daughter of PHRASIMUS and DIOGENEIA

ALCIPPE ——— **METION**

Daughter of ARES

Brother of CECROPS. King of Athens

DAEDALUS ——— **NAUCRATE**

A slave of King MINOS

ICARUS

139

MINOS, RHADAMANTHYS and SARPEDON were the three sons of the union between ZEUS and EUROPE. Following their birth, ZEUS arranged for EUROPE to marry the childless king of Crete, ASTERIUS, when the the three boys became heirs to the Cretan throne.

As young men, the three quarrelled over the love of a beautiful boy named MILETUS. The boy chose SARPEDON and as a result this pair were driven from Crete by MINOS. They went to Asia Minor, where the young boy founded the kingdom of Miletus.

On the death of their father, ASTERIUS, it was MINOS who claimed the throne and became a wise ruler, assisted by RHADAMANTHYS who instigated a just legal system. There were rivals for the throne, but MINOS said that, as a son of ZEUS, it was his by divine right and he went on to say that he could also ask the Gods for anything he wished. When challenged, he asked POSEIDON for a handsome bull which he promised to sacrifice to the God. His wish was granted when a wonderful white bull swam ashore and arrived at the palace, silencing his rivals for ever more. However, MINOS admired the bull so much that he put it with his herd and sacrificed one of his own bulls in its place. POSEIDON was not fooled. Angry at the insult, he got his revenge by making MINOS's wife, PASIPHAE, fall hopelessly in love with the white bull.

PASIPHAE's unnatural desire for the bull became an obsession and, to fulfill her overpowering lust, she turned to the famous architect, engineer and craftsman, the inventive DAEDALUS, for help. He solved the problem for her by constructing a life size, hollow, wooden cow, covering it with cow hide. PASIPHAE could gain entry through a door in the back of the construction, positioning herself inside its hollow, rear legs. The trick worked, PASIPHAE and the bull were satisfied, but from the union came a horrifying monster with a human body and bull's head, the dreadful MINOTAUR. As for the white bull, it grew more and more wild, ravaging the area round about the Cretan palace of Knossos. You may remember that it was the seventh labour of HERACLES, to capture it and it was finally killed in Marathon by THESEUS.

PASIPHAE was in disgrace and MINOS, not knowing how to hide her monstrous offspring, consulted the oracle, which said.' Instruct DAEDALUS to build you a retreat at Knossos.' The retreat which the architect constructed was to be known as the Labyrinth, an unfathomable maze whose centre had a chamber that housed the MINOTAUR.

As a ruler, MINOS rapidly expanded his domain, controlling the sea and most of the other kingdom in the region. The wise legislation of MINOS and RHADMANTHYS became legendary and a golden age of Cretan domination was born.

MINOS lived up to the reputation of his father, ZEUS, when it came to his love life. His affairs were countless and his jealous wife, PASIPHAE, arranged that he be bewitched. Instead of his seed, his mistresses were impregnated with poisonous vermin. It required the help of the sorceress, CIRCE, to provide him with an antidote.

Now one of MINOS's sons, ANDROGEUS, was killed on the orders of King AEGEUS of Athens, probably out of jealousy because the young man had taken most of the honours at the Panathenaic Games. His death led to MINOS declaring war on Athens and when that city proved to be impregnable he called for the help of the Gods. The Gods inflicted a plague on Athens which was eventually

lifted at great cost to the city, when, as
payment, it had to send, every nine years,
seven virgins and seven youths to the
Cretan palace to feed the MINOTAUR.
THESEUS, you may remember, killed the
MINOTAUR, with the help of DAEDALUS
and MINOS's daughter, ARIADNE.

DAEDALUS was punished for his part in
the killing of the MINOTAUR, MINOS
imprisoning him and his son, ICARUS, in
the labyrinth. The ingenious DAEDALUS,
however, built himself and his son a pair of
wings each, from feathers and wax and they
both made their escape by flying from the
labyrinth. DAEDALUS warned ICARUS

not to fly too low, or the spray from the ocean would wet the feathers, and not to fly too high, or the wax would melt from the heat of the sun. The unfortunate ICARUS did fly too high, the sun melted the wax and he fell into the Aegean Sea. His body was eventually washed up on an island where HERACLES found it, buried it and called the island Icaria.

As for DAEDALUS, he reached Sicily, where he lived in the court of King COCALUS.

Minos was determined to find DAEDALUS and instigated a search for him, far and wide. Knowing that the architect was likely to be living somewhere under royal protection, he conceived a plan whereby he sailed from port to port, asking the local kings if they could perform the task of threading a spiral sea shell, knowing that only DAEDALUS could solve the problem. When King COCALUS returned the shell duly threaded, MINOS knew that his search was over. He demanded that COCALUS hand DAEDALUS over and this the king agreed to do, after a feast that he would hold for his illustrious visitor. MINOS was made a guest in the royal palace and, while having a bath with the king's daughters in attendance, they poured boiling water on him, killing him.

Following his death, MINOS, in recognition of his skill as a counsellor and law enforcer, was made chief judge of the dead and advisor as to their fate, serving HADES along with his brother RHADAMANTHYS and AEACUS.

Part 12
THE DIOSCURI

ZEUS ——— **IO**

King of the Gods   *Daughter of INACHUS the Argive River God*

EPHASUS ——— **MEMPHIS**

Founds of Memphis   *Daughter of the God of the NILE*

POSEIDON ——— **LIBYA**

God of the Sea   *The Goddess of Libya*

AGENOR ——— **JOCASTA**

King of Sidon in Phoenicia   *Daughter of MENOECEUS a Thebian Noble*

ARES ——— **DEMONICE**

The God of War

THESTIUS ——— **EURYTHEMIS**

King of Aetolia

ZEUS ——— **LEDA** ——— **TYNDAREUS**

King of the Gods   *The Lady*   *King of Sparta*

HELEN   **CLYTAEMNESTRA**

Wife of MENELAUS   *Wife of AGAMEMNON*

POLYDEUCES   **CASTOR**

The DIOSCURI were twin boys called CASTOR and POLYDEUCES, the latter sometimes known as POLLUX. They had twin sisters, named HELEN and CLYTAEMNESTRA. Their father, TYNDAREUS, king of Sparta, had at one time married his own daughter, LEDA, who had four children by him. The birth was a complicated matter as LEDA had been seduced by ZEUS, who appeared to her in the form of a swan, on the same day that she had lain with TYNDAREUS. Two eggs were fertilized and it is generally accepted that HELEN and POLYDEUCES were from the seed of ZEUS, thus immortal, while CLYTAEMNESTRA and CASTOR were fathered by TYNDAREUS. It was HELEN who, when she eloped with PARIS, became the cause of the long and bitter seige of Troy, while

Zeus as a swan

CLYTAEMNESTRA became the murderous wife of AGAMEMNON, king of Mycenae.

The twin boys, inseparable throughout their numerous exploits, were known as the DIOSCURI and as we shall see, it was ordained by ZEUS that CASTOR would become immortal, like his brother. POLYDEUCES grew up to be the finest boxer in the land, while CASTOR was famed for his skill as a tamer of horses, also excelling as a soldier. They both received many prizes for their victories in the Olympic Games. They took part in the famous hunt for the Calydonian Boar and served with distinction on the Argo, in the quest for the Golden Fleece, during which journey, you may recall, POLYDEUCES not only won the boxing contest against King AMYCUS, but also killed that bully with a mighty final blow.

When THESEUS and his companion PIRITHOUS abducted HELEN from Sparta and took her to Athens, it was the cunning and resolve of the twins that ensured the rescue of their sister and they made sure that they timed the action to coincide with a period when THESEUS was away on one of his many exploits. They raided Athens with an army recruited from Sparta and Arcadia, captured the city, took THESEUS' mother prisoner and put MENESTHEUS on the throne. It spelled the end of the reign of THESEUS who was exiled on his return, shortly afterwards to be murdered by King LYCOMEDES.

When the DIOSCURI wanted wives, they abducted their cousins, PHOEBE and HILAEIRA, who were the daughters of the brother of King TYNDAREUS. Now it so happened that the two girls were already betrothed to LYNCEUS and IDAS, another set of twins and also cousins of the DIOSCURI. It was this affair that made the two sets of twins sworn enemies and matters came to a head when they were jointly involved in a raid to steal a large herd of cattle. Instead of the spoils being divided four ways, the DIOSCURI were cheated of their share, which LYNCEUS and IDAS took to Messenia.

The DIOSCURI, with a Spartan army, raided Messenia and recovered the cattle, only to be pursued by their cousins. So they hid in a hollow oak tree in order to ambush them. Unfortunately, LYNCEUS was gifted with the ability to see hidden objects and soon detected the DIOSCURI in their hiding place. IDAS threw a spear at the oak tree and transfixed CASTOR, who died immediately. POLYDEUCES retaliated by killing LYNCEUS with his spear and ZEUS protected his immortal son by disposing of IDAS with a thunderbolt.

POLYDEUCES. the remaining twin, implored his father ZEUS to let him join his beloved brother CASTOR. ZEUS granted his brave son his wish, making CASTOR immortal and placing the two Heroes in the sky where today they can be seen as the Heavenly Twins, the GEMINI.

Part 13

MELEAGER

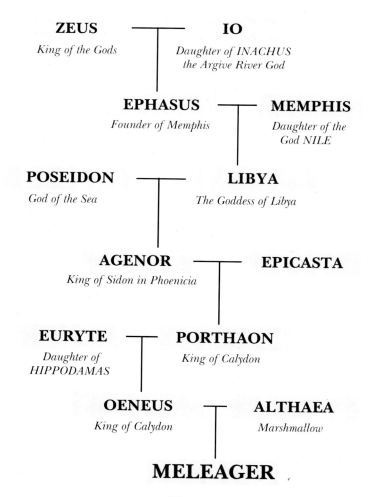

ZEUS

King of the Gods

IO

*Daughter of INACHUS
the Argive River God*

EPHASUS

Founder of Memphis

MEMPHIS

*Daughter of the
God NILE*

POSEIDON

God of the Sea

LIBYA

The Goddess of Libya

AGENOR

King of Sidon in Phoenicia

EPICASTA

EURYTE

*Daughter of
HIPPODAMAS*

PORTHAON

King of Calydon

OENEUS

King of Calydon

ALTHAEA

Marshmallow

MELEAGER

MELEAGER was the son of King OENEUS of Calydon, an area on the south west of the Greek mainland, his mother being ALTHAEA. Just after he was born, his mother was visited by the three MOERAE, also known as the FATES. They were both birth spirits and death spirits who decided a person's lot in life, the word MOERAE meaning 'allotted portions'. They were known as CLOTHO, LACHESIS and ATROPOS who respectively spun the thread of life, decided its quality and cut it at the chosen time. CLOTHO and LACHESIS told Althaea that her son would be noble and brave, but ATROPOS told her that he would die as soon as a stick, which was burning in the grate, was consumed by the flames of the fire. ALTHAEA quickly extinguished the stick and hid it in the palace.

As MELEAGER grew up it was soon evident that he was outstandingly courageous and was the best javelin thrower in all Greece. In fact, he was just a young boy when he joined JASON on the Argo in the quest for the Golden Fleece and some say that it was MELEAGER who killed the arch enemy of the Argonauts, King AEETES of Colchis. On his return from the adventure, he married CLEOPATRA, the daughter of IDAS, and one of the twin rivals of the DIOSCURI.

Now it so happened that MELEAGER'S father, OENEUS, failed to include ARTEMIS in his annual sacrifices to the great Olympian Gods and as a punishment she sent a fearsome wild boar to Calydon. It ravaged the crops and killed many people. So OENEUS invited the most courageous fighters in Greece to form a hunting party, with a prize of the boar's tusks and hide for the successful slayer of the beast.

The Calydonian
Boar Hunt

An impressive array of Heroes answered
the call, (see illustration) together with a
Heroine, the virgin huntress ATALANTA,
the daughter of IASUS, the king of Tegea.
IASUS had only wanted sons so when a girl
was born he left the baby to die in a forest.
The Goddess of Hunting, ARTEMIS,
directed a bear to suckle the child, after
which she was found by a tribe of hunters
who brought her up as one of them. She
chose to remain a virgin so that nothing
could interfere with her love of hunting
and her fame spread as a swift footed and
highly skilled huntress. You may recall that
she joined JASON on the Argo.

When the hunting party assembled there was some dissension, especially from ANCAEUS and CEPHEUS, who did not want to be in the company of a woman, but MELEAGER, who was captivated by the beautiful ATALANTA, threatened to call off the expedition if she was not included. His love for ATALANTA offended his family, especially his mother and her four brothers, who were on the side of CLEOPATRA. Bad feeling was already brewing which, you can be sure, was partly generated by ARTEMIS. The hunt for the Calydonian Boar, as it had been named, began by the light of the moon. Armed with boar spears, javelins, axes, bows and arrows, the hunters spread out and advanced slowly through the forest which the boar was known to inhabit. The first blood to be shed was human blood when ATALANTA slew two Centaurs, who had joined the party, when they attempted to rape her. She continued on the hunt at MELEAGER's side. The boar was flushed out from its lair and, killing two of the hunters, it chased NESTOR up a tree. JASON's javelin was off target, as was the spear of IPHICLES. PELEUS and TELEMON almost came to grief, saved only by the timely arrow of ATALANTA, which pierced the ear of the wild boar. ANCAEUS taunted ATALANTA for not delivering a fatal shot and he attacked the beast with his axe. The boar was too quick for him and killed him, sinking its great tusks into his body, disembowelling and castrating him. Accidentally, a badly aimed javelin of PELEUS killed his companion hunter, EURYTION. At length it was AMPHIARAUS whose arrow pierced the eye of the boar; the enraged animal almost took THESEUS unawares but finally MELEAGER successfully speared its flank and, writhing in pain, the boar was slain by his second thrust which found the creature's heart.

MELEAGER skinned the beast and presented its hide to

ATALANTA because, he said, she had been the first to draw blood, but this upset many of the party, who felt the hide should go to MELEAGER. It was two of his uncles who protested the loudest because of their hatred of ATALANTA and the enraged MELEAGER killed them both. His mother, on seeing her dead brothers, remembered the words of ATROPOS, the FATE who cut the thread of life. She took the charred stick from its hiding place and threw it on the fire whereupon poor MELEAGER died an agonising death. He was mourned by his sisters and all the women of the palace. The vengeful ARTEMIS was not finished however. She turned the sorrowful women into guinea fowl.

In Conclusion

In researching the Heroes we ourselves have come to love
heroic HERACLES, courageous THESEUS, fearless
PERSEUS, resolute JASON, rash BELLEROPHON, valiant
ACHILLES, long suffering ODYSSEUS, talented
ORPHEUS, royal AGAMEMNON, determined ORESTES,
tragic OEDIPUS, cunning MINOS, ingenious DAEDALUS,
the daring DIOSCURI and the sporting MELEAGER.
Their characters were often in question, good and bad,
cruel and kind, fair and foul, generous and mean but
always half human.

There are many other, lesser Heroes and Heroines whose
feats we have not been able to include in this volume, but
we hope that we have achieved our aim, that is, to whet the
appetite and that you, our reader, will wish to delve deeper
into the mysteries of Greek Mythology. Perhaps, as we
have, you will begin to feel that some or all of these
characters really existed and crossed that thin line between
Gods and mortals, between fantasy and fact. The tales of
their epic feats were handed down orally, probably
embellished to make them even more entertaining and it
would not be surprising if the story teller occasionally wove
some local news into his narrative, but was there a thread of
truth running through it?